A *Golden Hands* PATTERN BOOK

HANDCRAFTS

A *Golden Hands* PATTERN BOOK

HANDCRAFTS

RANDOM HOUSE   NEW YORK

Photographers:

Pages 7, 16, 17, 21, 22, 23, 87, 110, 115, 116, 117, 121 John Carter / 10, 11, 22, 23, 24, 25, 26, 28, 29, 41, 43, 44, 46, 47, 64, 80, 81, 85, 93, 98, 100, 101, 113, 118, 119 Chris Lewis / 37, 38 Steve Bicknell / 42, 84, 86, 103, 104, 107, 122 Bruce Scott / 50 Peter Watkins / 51 Adele Baker / 54, 55 Roger Charity / 63 Michael Boys / 92, 94 Bill McLaughlin / 120 Anne Maille / 127 Joy Simpson / 30, 33, 108 Malcolm Aird / 62 Paul Redman / 109 Renee Robinson.

Illustrators:

Pages 8, 95 Barbara Firth / 14, 15 A. Edwards / 19, 20, 115 Janet Ahlberg / 27, 45, 64, 65, 66, 87, 112, 114, 118, 119, 124, 125, 126 Paul Williams.

Designers:

Pages 6 Evelyn Samuel / 19 Pat Webb necklet and belt / 21 Kelly Flynn bracelet and rings / 22 Caroline de Bethel chokers / 23 F. Dixon and R. Hoogstrahn belt, bracelet and necklace / 38 John Crawford pendant / 41 earrings and pendant / 48 Frances Kay / 49, 50 Eiran Short / 51 Marjorie Self / 54, 55 Anna Griffiths / 62 Barbara Tuck / 64, 65 Angela Fishburn / 74 Bruce Angrave / 93 Sara Fitzgerald / 98–100 Selina Thomas bag and sandals / 113 Betty Docherty / 115 Sylvia Gifford patchwork waistcoat, belt and bag / 120 Anna Cloote loom / 127 weaving samples.

Picture credits:

Pages 12 Scala / 58, 59, 60 Photo Text / 68 Conway Picture Library / 82, 83 Search Press / 123 Femina.

Acknowledgements:

Pages 7 Batik designs by Evelyn Samuel from 'Introducing Batik' published by Batsford Ltd. / 39, 40 Stage pictures from John Crawford's 'Introducing Jewellery Making' published by Batsford Ltd. / 52, 53 The panel 'Street of Houses' by Patricia Redding is from her book 'Collage' / 75 Water lilies reproduced by permission of Mappin and Webb. / 76 Penguin reproduced by permission of Spicer Cowan (Penguin Papers); policeman reproduced by permission of Odhams Press Ltd. / 78 Globe Theatre reproduced by permission of the Central Office of Information. / 75, 79 Folding and cutting projects from Paper Sculpture by Arthur Aadler published by Blandford Press. / 96, 97 Pictures by Pamela McDowall from her book 'Pressed Flower Collage' published by Littlewood Press.

Originally published in Great Britain by Marshall Cavendish Limited under the title *The Golden Hands Book of Popular Crafts in 1973.*

Library of Congress Cataloging in Publication Data
Main entry under title:
Handcrafts: a Golden hands pattern book.
1. Handicraft.   I. Golden hands.
TT157.H323   745.5   73-5016
ISBN 0-394-48796-6

Manufactured in Great Britain
First American Edition

CONTENTS

Batik

A modern interpretation worked on pure silk in five colours

Batik is an Indonesian word describing a form of resist printing which is obtained when hot wax, an effective resist to dye, is applied to fabric. When the fabric is dyed, only the unwaxed areas of the cloth take the colour. Multicoloured patterns are achieved by rewaxing and redyeing different parts of the design, and fine lines are made using a tjanting, which is a tool for applying hot wax. Dyeing is carried out in cool water to prevent the wax from melting. Although batik printing is practised mainly in Java and in Indonesia, resist printing and dyeing with wax are also known in India, Africa, and parts of Europe. In the western world, batik has become a popular craft and can be done at home using simple domestic equipment, with the exception of the tjanting tool, which is purchased from specialist craft shops.

Equipment and Materials

For waxing you will need:

A double saucepan for melting wax (or a saucepan and a tin to contain the wax, which can be placed in the pan).

A gas ring or electric hotplate—standing on a piece of asbestos if possible, as a safety precaution.

Wax, in the form of domestic candles or blocks of paraffin wax purchased from chemists and specialist craft shops. Powdered wax is also available. Beeswax, which is more expensive, provides the most flexible wax.

Artists' brushes for applying wax—medium sized for outlining areas, large sized for filling in large areas.

Tjanting tool. Resin powder.

Old picture frame. Drawing pins.

A flat table surface.

Quantity of old newspaper.

For dyeing:

A plastic or enamel bowl to hold the dye mixture.

A plastic or glass measure, for water.

Rubber gloves.

Polythene sheeting, to protect table while dyed material dries.

Plastic spoons of various sizes, for spooning out dyes.

Small plastic containers for mixing dyes.

Cold water dyes.

Protective clothing.

Nylon clothes line and clothes pegs.

Fabrics for batik

Best results are obtained on cotton, cotton lawn, calico, silk and linen, also on mixtures of wool and cotton. Man-made fibres and materials with special finishes, such as crease-resistant, non-iron or drip dry fabrics, are not suitable for beginners as the dyes do not penetrate these surfaces easily.

Designs for batik

Some very effective patterns can be made by designs based on the circle, the square or the triangle. Natural objects such as stones, shells, bark seed leaves and plants all offer a starting point and the designs will develop almost on their own as the dyeing and waxing progresses.

Museum visits are a good opportunity to study patterns used by primitive peoples on their pottery, weapons and carvings. And photographs of buildings, stacks of building materials, bricks, pavements, drain covers, roofs and stones all provide a basis of pleasing colours, shapes and patterns which can be adapted for use on textiles.

Preparing for waxing

Before dyeing, the cloth must be washed thoroughly to remove all traces of dressing, sizes and natural oils. When the material is ironed free of creases, it is ready for the application of wax resist.

Preparing the wax

Cut up or grate the candles or pieces cut from a block of wax and melt in a double saucepan over heat. It should be emphasised that when handling hot wax great care must be taken at all times. A more flexible, less brittle wax is obtained by adding one part of resin to four parts of paraffin wax.

Applying the wax

The wax must be kept hot while you are working and there are two basic methods of applying it. It can be painted on, using a brush, varying the size according to the area to be waxed. For fine lines and for textured effects, a tjanting is used. There are two ways of working when applying wax. The material can be simply spread out flat on layers of newspaper, and this is the method used when large areas of fabric are being treated. As the wax passes through the fabric, it cools and adheres to the paper beneath. As the fabric is peeled off for dyeing, the wax inevitably cracks and this can cause bleeding of dyeing, which may not be part of the design. Beginners will probably find it more satisfactory to work with the fabric pinned to a frame. An old picture frame will do. The tjanting is dipped into the hot wax, filling the reservoir, and is then carried to the prepared fabric. To prevent the wax from dripping hold a piece of paper under the spout. Hold the tjanting in the right hand immediately above the surface of the fabric and move it along the design lines.

Providing the wax is hot enough, a fine trail of wax will flow from the spout. As the wax penetrates the fabric appears to go transparent. Remember, wax is applied only to those areas which are not going to be dyed.

Batik dyeing

The secret of successful batik dyeing is a large enough container, so that the waxed fabric can be moved around without undue crushing.

Follow the manufacturers' instructions for preparing the dye, and make sure that the solution is quite cool before starting dyeing or the wax will melt and destroy the design. If the wax is cracked the dye will run in, and a fine marbling texture will result. This effect is sometimes used for background to designs. After dyeing is completed, drain the fabric off by laying it flat on several sheets of newspaper spread on a table top. Polythene sheeting under the newspaper will prevent any dye from staining through to the table top. After it has drained, the fabric can be hung up to dry. It is then ready for waxing further areas of the design. After two applications of wax and dye, boil off the wax and start again. This is very important because dye chemicals cause a deterioration in the wax and dye can penetrate the fabric in areas which should be free of dye.

This process of waxing and cold dyeing is repeated until as many colours have been applied as required.

Removing the wax

There are two methods of removing wax. The first is by boiling the wax out of the fabric. Heat the water in a large saucepan and when the water is boiling put in the waxed fabric and gently move it about with a wooden spoon for not more than three minutes. Lift the fabric out and drop it into a bucket of cold water. The wax will solidify immediately. After squeezing out the water, shake off the loose wax. Add half a teaspoonful of detergent to the boiling water and repeat this process twice, or until there is no trace of wax left. Finally, wash and dry the fabric in the usual way. If a small quantity of wax persists in the fabric, professional dry cleaning will remove the residue. The waxy water must never be poured down a sink, as it will cause a blockage. Wait until the water cools, then remove the crust of wax on the surface of the water and pour the clear water away. The wax cannot be used again because the dye chemicals have probably deteriorated it.

Points to watch

The technique of batik printing is straight

forward, but while you are learning you may experience one or two disappointments. Here are some points to watch to help you to achieve the best results.

Bleeding of colour under the wax. This can happen if the wax is not hot enough to penetrate the fabric, or if the wax is damaged as the waxed fabric is pulled off the newspaper. It's best to use a frame.

Blurred edges to the design. This will result if the dye solution is warm and the waxed design softened. Make sure the dye is cool.

Blurred designs and muddied colours. This will result if the fabric is left to boil too long when boiling out the wax. The loose dye in the water can be re-absorbed.

Pale Colours. If the dye is not sufficiently fixed before the wax is boiled off, the colour may wash out and be too pale. Allow the dye to dry thoroughly first. If you are not pleased with the result of waxing and dyeing, the majority of cold dyes can be removed by boiling the fabric in a solution of colour remover.

The tjanting, used for applying melted wax, is held just above the surface of the fabric ▼

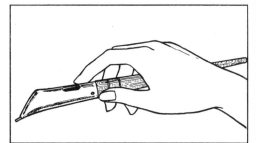

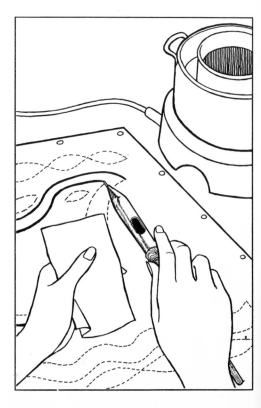

Two yards of white pure silk fabric are required to make this brilliantly coloured batik printed lampshade, and four dyeings are needed to produce the effect—brilliant yellow, followed by bright red, bright blue and finally, navy blue. The brilliance and clarity of the colours in this example is achieved by the use of single colour in some areas, and this necessitated removing all the wax after each dye process. The wax was then re-applied to the entire surface, except those areas where a pure, single colour was required. A certain amount of crackle has been allowed on the background colour by immersing the waxed fabric in warm water before the last dyeing. The four stages of dyeing are shown here: top left, the first

colour, yellow; top right, red ; bottom left, blue; bottom right, navy blue. Whether cotton, linen or silk fabric is used, the material must be cleaned of all dressings and oils before batik printing is started. Silk fabric should be soaked in a hot soapless detergent solution for about an hour and cotton should be boiled for about half an hour. Rinse carefully and hang the fabric to dry to minimise creasing. When the material is dry, draw the design out in pencil—the design shown here is based on a simple geometric repeat—and then stretch the fabric across a frame before waxing. Special frames can be purchased but a picture frame will do should you prefer to use one.

Bead jewellery

Beads in fashion

Decorative beads have played an important part in sophisticated fashion for centuries. Archaeological finds in Egypt have uncovered ancient glass beads, beautifully shaped, and medieval women wore elaborate bead ornaments in their hair. Among the American Indians bead work was a major art, and their bold designs have influenced many contemporary fashions. In the nineteenth century, Victorian ladies made small beaded accessories as a home craft. Bead jewellery, or some

Elaborate bead jewellery was proudly displayed by every medieval lady of quality and distinction

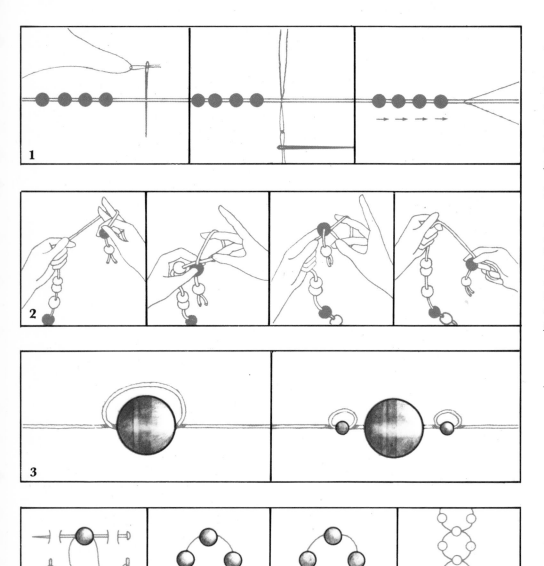

Threading small beads
Sometimes, small beads are sold strung on thread. If you break the thread the tiny beads spring apart. A useful tip is illustrated in diagram 1. Thread a needle with cotton thread and pass the necklace thread through the loop of the cotton. Pierce the thread supporting the beads with the needle and pull the thread through. Hold the new bead thread parallel with the old and slide bead across.

Bead knotting
When beads are to be spaced from each other either for appearance or for safety of precious stones, the simple knotting technique here is used. If thread seems too visible, a small bead is strung both sides of a large bead, the thread being strung through the small bead twice. On nylon, if small beads are threaded about 2 inches apart using this method, a pretty effect is achieved. Diagrams 2, 3 ◄ ▼

Jeweller's findings
For some necklaces a metal clasp is needed for finishing and fastening. After a necklace or bracelet is finished, the thread ends are taken under the tongue and the back of the clasp and then taken up through the last two beads. Many different kinds of findings are available, some of them with perforated surfaces so that smaller beads can be stitched on. (Not illustrated.)

Two-thread technique
This is the basic technique of beadwork and can be used with endless variations. Take a long thread and run it through a single bead. Push a pin through the bead and fix that to a cushion pad. Now working with both ends of the thread, thread a bead on the left hand thread and another on the right hand thread. Cross the threads through the fourth bead and proceed as before. Diagram 4 ◄

form of decoration made from beads, has never been out of fashion for long, whether the feeling has been for the recent simple string of pearls or, by contrast, the heavy Victorian jet collars. Today, with current trends towards soft, informal clothes, beads are a natural accessory. In this chapter some, but by no means all, of the techniques of bead stringing are illustrated. The effects created can be as varied as the imagination and taste of the individual designer —from massive, sparkling necklaces to a single understated medallion on a leather thong.

Materials for beadwork can often be found just lying about, waiting for a sharp-eyed collector, although speciality shops can be an equally good source for discovering beautiful, expensive beads.

Materials and equipment

Beads
Almost anything through which a hole can be bored can be used as a bead: shells, seeds, fruit pips, sweet smelling spices such as cloves and cardomom, nut shells, kernels, dried berries, animal and fish teeth, pieces of bone, scraps of leather, pieces of wood—all these have been successfully used for decorative jewellery.

More formal and familiar beads are usually either round, oval, square, raindrop or baton shaped and are made of precious and semi-precious stones, mineral substances, coral and jet, glass and crystal, porcelain, pottery, plastics and resins. Beads are obtainable in large or small quantities from craft shops, needlework shops and specialist suppliers.

Start a collection of beads for jewellery making—it can be like searching for treasure. Chain store jewellery counters provide a variety of inexpensive bead necklaces which can be broken up and reassembled. Junk shops and second hand clothing shops are worth searching for beautiful old beads which are now becoming scarce, and elderly lady friends can be counted on to have a broken bracelet or brooch tucked away. A single beautiful bead can be used as the centerpiece of a brooch and is well worth looking for.

Threads and strings
A variety of different threads and strings can be used for making bead jewellery, depending on the design and the size of bead being used.

Bead silk, strong twist thread, Perlon and Trevira thread, various weights of nylon thread, thin cords and wire are among

Bead mosaic

The diagrams here show how close dense surfaces are built up. A row of beads is strung fairly loosely and then the thread is taken back through the last bead but one. A new bead is taken up each time, the thread going back through the second bead of the row before. This principle can be used with cord, nylon thread or wire. Pretty medallions, earrings and pendants can be made. Diagram 5 ►

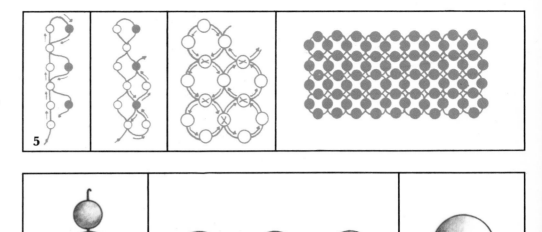

Working with wire

Working with wire, three dimensional effects are possible. A pair of pliers is needed for this kind of bead work. The illustrations show how wire is bent into links for beads and how beads are secured by wire. For a dropping bead, for a pendant or an earring, a jeweller's pin is used. To hold a large bead securely at the end of a drop, the wire is threaded through a smaller bead. Diagrams 6, 7 ► ▼

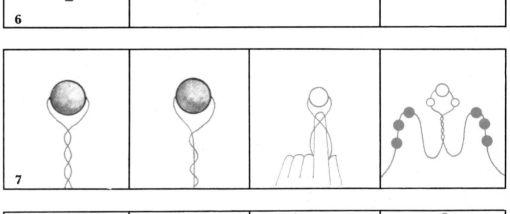

Alternative finishing

If a different kind of finishing is required, the simplest is a bar and ring made of beads. Knot the threads through a bar bead and finish the ends through six beads making a circle. Glue the ends of the threads before passing them through the last bead. The glue will adhere to the inside of the bead and hold it securely out of sight. Use this method for finishing off thread ends (Not illustrated.)

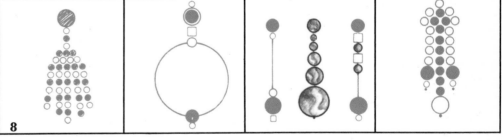

Pendant earrings

Here are some ideas for pendant earrings. A small flat backed bead is used to hide the metal finish of the earclip. Alternatively, glue a piece of fabric or leather to the clip and either cover it with beads or leave it plain. Wooden beads can be split to make half beads by tapping a tack into the hole. Paint them with shiny enamel paint or nail polish ►

those most commonly used, but leather thongs, thick cords and macramé twine are also used for some types of jewellery. Dental floss, obtainable from most chemists, is also recommended.

Wire for jewellery making is available in soft copper, brass or silver. Copper plated steel wire is also used and is easy to work. Wire is available in a range of gauges. Florist's wire can be used for some techniques in jewellery making.

Needles

Long thin beading needles are useful for threading beads with small holes, and needles of different gauges can be used as long as the eye will pass through the bead. Some threads are stiff enough to be passed through a bead without a needle, and other threads can be dipped in glue or twisted with soap to stiffen the ends.

For working with wire a pair of pointed, half-round pliers, a pair of side cutters for cutting wire and a fine file are needed.

Clasps and fastenings

Clasps and fastenings for jewellery are called 'findings' and are obtainable from specialist suppliers and crafts shops in a wide and varied range of styles.

Pins and working pad

For more intricate bead work, such as mosaic beading, a working pad similar to that used in lace making is advised, a felt-covered brick or a piece of cork mat covered in felt will do. Long, glass headed pins are used for holding bead patterns in position during working.

A felt or velvet lined tray is ideal for making most other kinds of jewellery. The design can be laid out in the tray without

the beads rolling about, and if the fabric is of a dark colour the colour contrasts show up more clearly. A few small plastic pots near the work tray will conveniently hold beads while they are being worked.

Techniques

Apart from the simple threading and knotting techniques used in single strand necklaces, there are other techniques in bead jewellery making which are more complex and require practice to perfect.

Mosaic beading, for instance, is rather similar to lace making and there are several variations on the basic patterns for achieving different effects. These are some of the techniques illustrated in this chapter and after a while, you will be able to identify which have been used to produce this beautiful jewellery.

for macramé necklace
☐ 4oz cone fine white macramé twine
☐ 24 long beads
☐ 20 round beads

To make the necklace
Lay four lengths of twine together to form holding cords. Set on twenty-four doubled threads across the center of these holding cords.

Thread on beads as shown, working a flat knot above the eight center beads and below all twelve beads. Thread on beads in the sequence illustrated, separating them with flat knots and ending each column with an overhand knot.

Complete the neckband of the necklace by working flat knots on either side of the beads to give the required length to fit around the neck.

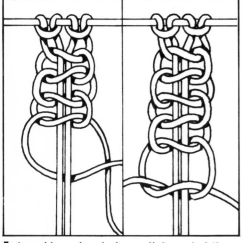

▼ *A necklace that looks as light and delicate as a cluster of raindrops— easily made by stringing together glass beads of different shapes and sizes*

▲ *A white macramé necklace with amber, red and white flat wooden beads*
▼ *Large and small beads strung closely together to make a solid necklace*

▲ Different effects can be achieved using small coloured beads or shells
▼ Eye-catching huge wooden beads look good strung on leather thongs

▲ Cord of different colours can be used as a contrast to the beads
▼ The variety of designs using toning and blending colours is endless

17

Bead weaving

Although the earliest beads used for woven bead jewellery and garments might well have been seeds, and the loom most likely a few pieces of stick, the craft of beadweaving is certainly a very ancient one. It is a traditional folk-craft in the north of South America, where the women weave themselves intricately patterned bead aprons, and was well-known to the North American Indians. Two forms of bead weaving are covered in this chapter. One uses a loom and produces a woven ribbon of beads. The other uses a cord-knotting technique to produce larger pieces of bead work which can be used to make jewellery and accessories.

Materials and equipment

Very little equipment is required for bead weaving. To produce a flat ribbon of closely woven beads a bead loom is essential.

Wood beading looms are inexpensive to buy, or they can be constructed from a wooden box with tacks hammered into it. Even a cardboard box with notches cut in the edges can be used as a loom, but threads must be stretched very tightly before work is begun, and only very small pieces of beadweaving can be worked by this method.

Beads. Small embroidery beads made of plastic, ceramic or glass, wooden coloured beads and natural wooden beads of all sizes can be used for weaving.

Needles. Long, thin beading needles, fine enough to go through the beads twice, are best.

Thread. This also must be fine enough to go twice through the beads. Either linen carpet thread or special beading cotton are recommended. If neither of these are available, thin crochet cotton may be used, but nylon thread must not be used as it is too rigid.

Designs for bead weaving

Beginners will find it easier to follow a chart, but after a little practice you will be able to work a simple design without having to follow a pattern. You can make a chart yourself on graph paper, when each small square will represent one bead of your design. Colour the squares with the colours of the beads you intend to use—this makes it much easier to follow a pattern. Charts for canvas work or cross stitch can be used for bead weaving and one bead will replace each stitch marked. If you are inventing your own pattern, start with an uncomplicated design, working up into more ambitious, three or four colour patterns. When creating a design for bead work, remember that curved lines have to be built up row by row, just as in canvas work.

After planning a design, work a few trial rows first, and count how many beads you will need for the completed work.

This charming bead picture 'Townscape' is a modern interpretation of the craft

Setting up the loom

The lengthwise stretched threads are known as the warp, and the beads lie between them, so the distance between the threads should correspond to the size of the beads you are using. There must always be one more warp thread than there are beads in the width of the pattern, and to give added strength to the edge of the weaving the two outside warp threads should be doubled. Therefore, if your pattern is 20 beads wide, you will need to stretch up 23 threads.

For a thin belt you can use as few as 10 beads across the pattern, but for a bag made of small beads you will need more threads and beads to give you the correct width.

Cut the warp threads to the length of beading you require plus 6 inches. Knot these threads in bunches of 5 round the square stick at the end of the loom, stretch them tightly across the combs, and secure them at the other end of the loom in the slot. You will find it quicker to keep beads of different colours separated in small, shallow containers. Small plastic boxes with lids can be bought and these are ideal. Sprinkle a few beads onto a piece of felt, ready to be picked up.

Beginning to weave

Thread the needle with the working thread, and attach the end of it to the double stretched thread on the left. Don't make the working thread too long, as it tangles easily. 15 inches is long enough. Work four rows without beads in darning stitch to make the top of the weaving firm, finishing on the left. Thread onto the working thread the beads required for the first row of the pattern, counting the pattern from the left.

This string of beads is now placed underneath the warp threads so that one bead is positioned under and between each two warp threads.

Press the string of beads up between the threads with the first finger of your left hand. Pass the needle from right to left back through the hole of each of the beads, thus securing them. Pull the thread fairly tight at the end of the row to make it firm, but be sure to keep the tension even because the edges of the weaving can easily become distorted. Begin the second row of the pattern working from the left again, and continue in this way until you have finished the pattern. Pull the thread back and forth through the previous rows every now and then for added strength.

If you happen to leave a warp thread exposed by mistake don't worry, it will be captured by the next line of beads.

To make long articles, first weave the length of the loom, then, loosening the warp threads from the slot, wind the weaving round the square stick, and then stretch the newly exposed threads.

Tighten the warp and proceed as before.

Finishing off

Work two or three lines of darning without beads with the last working thread, then take the working thread back through the last row but one of the beads. Tie a knot and cut the thread.

Lift the warp threads off the loom, take two warp threads at a time back through the beads, knot again, then cut. Run the knots up to the beads on a pin.

Fancy finishes

To make a five-bead side fringe.

Tie the working thread on the left-hand double warp threads, and thread on a row of beads in the usual way, according to the pattern, but add five extra beads for the side fringe. When turning at the end of the row, ignore the number five bead, but thread the working thread back through the four fringe beads, then work through the pattern beads in the normal way. For a fringe at both sides, as soon as the pattern beads have been worked through thread on five extra beads, turn, ignore the first bead but thread the working thread back through the four extra beads. Thread on the pattern beads and continue.

To make up a side U loop (Five beads)

Tie the working thread on the left-hand double warp threads and thread a row of beads in the usual way, according to the pattern. Add on an extra five beads, then, without turning, thread on another row of pattern beads. Press up these two rows of pattern beads and catch them with the working thread, starting from the left-hand warp for the first row, and going back as usual from the right-hand warp for the second row. Ignore the extra five beads at the end and they will form a loop. If you want a side U loop at both sides of the work, at the end of these two rows add an extra five beads, thread on your pattern beads, add five extra beads, thread on the pattern beads, and then catch these two rows of pattern beads, ignoring the extra five at each end, which will form loops.

For a longer loop, thread on more extra beads. For a scalloped edge, add three extra beads only.

Top: two different hand-made looms
1. *Pressing beads up between warp threads*
2. *Passing needle back through the beads*

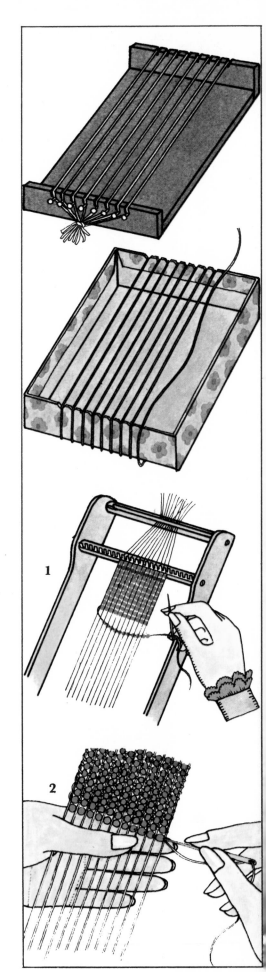

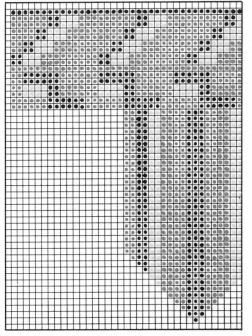

Chart for the three-colour necklet—top right   *Chart for the fringed bracelet—bottom right*

▲ *Complete necklet's panel and remove work
from loom. Hand-thread beads onto six pairs of
threads on left and right, cut central five
threads to 2ins and thread back into work.
Proceed with side strips to pattern shown above.*

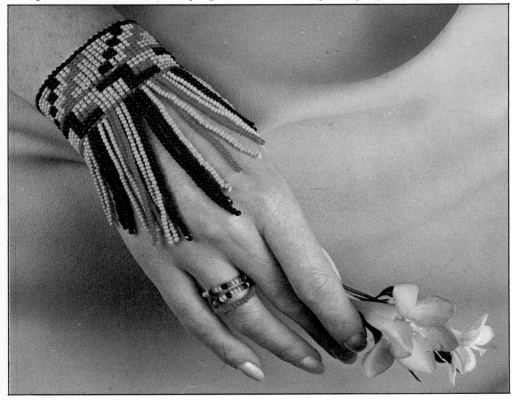

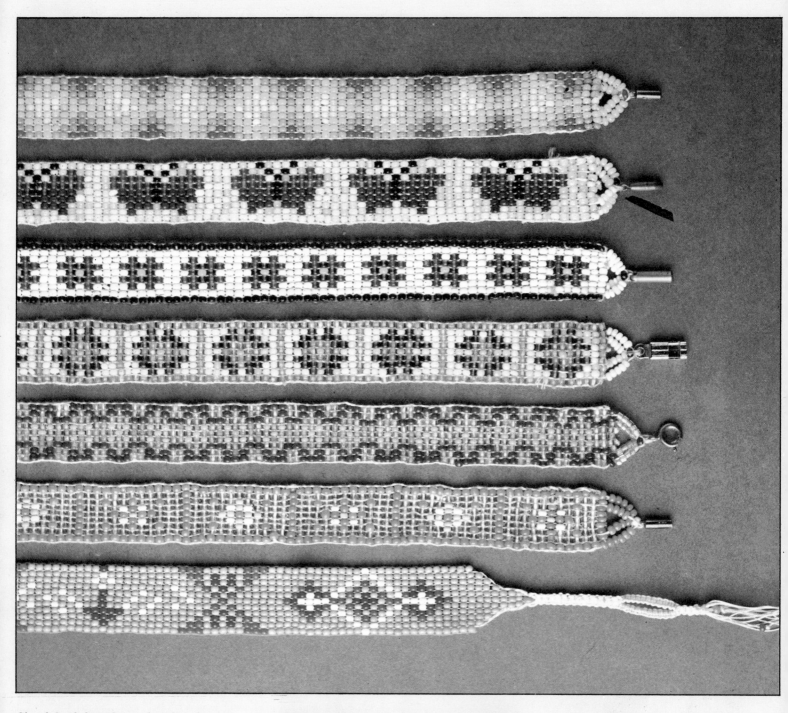

Six of the chokers shown above have been finished off with conventional necklace fastenings, the threads worked back through the last few beads before knotting off. The lower necklet and the belt on the right have been finished with macramé flat knots with additional beads interthreaded. To make a macramé flat knot on four threads follow the diagram and work as follows: pass the left thread under the center two threads and over the right hand thread to form a loop. Pick up the end of the right hand thread and pass it from front to back through the loop and draw it up tightly. This forms a half knot. Now pass the right hand thread under the center threads and over the left hand thread and put the end of left hand thread through loop for a flat knot.

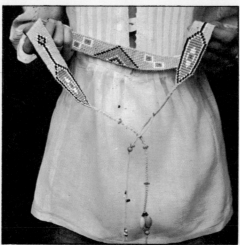

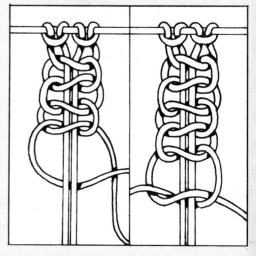

22

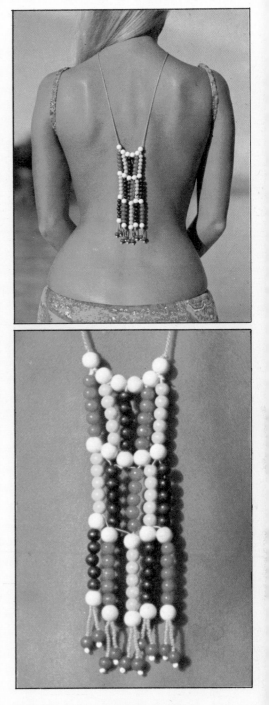

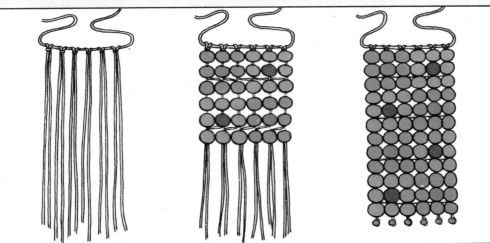

▲ The two belts and the pendant illustrated are made by various cord-knotting techniques which can also be used for making large beadwork items such as vests. The diagrams show one pattern of cord-knotting. Knot six thin cords onto a thicker cord, using a macramé knot. Dip the ends of the thin cord into melted candle wax to make bead threading easier. Thread beads onto the pairs of cords. After two rows of beads have been threaded, working from the left, string the first bead onto a single cord, and take its pair across to the second bead. Take one of the second beads' cords across to the third bead and so on to the last bead which has three cords through it. After two more rows, take the cords back across again.

Candles

Original candles

Using quite simple equipment and a lot of imagination, an almost infinite variety of candle shapes can be made. Some of the ideas in this chapter are beautiful and some are astonishing — such as the water candles above.

Materials and equipment

Assemble the materials before starting work. A candlemakers supplier will stock most of them.

You will need:

☐ Paraffin wax
☐ Beeswax sheets (for beeswax candles)
☐ Stearin
☐ Wax dyes
☐ Candle perfumes (if perfumed candles are required)
☐ Wicks
☐ Sugar thermometer
☐ Two large saucepans: one is for melting wax, the other for dissolving colour
☐ Enamel jug with a lip for pouring molten wax

☐ Deep enamel jug for making dipped candles
☐ Mould seal (plasticine or clay)
☐ Ruler
☐ Wicking needle (to make holes for wicks)
☐ Deep receptacle for cold water
☐ Moulds
☐ Spoons for ladling molten wax
☐ Sand, for sand casting, in a box

Paraffin wax. The types of paraffin wax available vary widely, but is recommended that a fully refined wax with a melting point of 135°-140°F be used. This type of paraffin wax is available from candle-makers suppliers in solid blocks or in a powdered form, which may be more convenient.

Wicks. Candlewicks are made of bleached linen thread and these are woven and graded to burn a certain area of wax. Wicks are usually sold in packs and sized according to the diameter of the candle they will successfully burn. A 1 inch wick will burn a candle 1 inch in diameter, and it will also burn a 1 inch

hole in a larger candle. It is therefore essential to use the correct size of wick; a large candle with a small wick looks very nice when burning—until the wick drowns in a pool of wax.

Wax dyes. Candles can be left white or coloured with dye—wax dyes are the best for the job. These are available in either powder or solid form. It is advisable to test dyes carefully, as too much dye will diminish the candle's glow. Test by taking a spoonful of the coloured candle wax and putting it in cold water. As it sets you will get an idea of the final shade. For most colours a tiny pinch of powdered dye will colour a pint of liquid wax.

Stearin. Dye is dissolved first in stearin—a white, flaky type of wax which allows the dye to dissolve readily and completely with perfect colour suspension. The proportion added is 10 per cent stearin to wax.

Thermometer. A sugar thermometer with readings up to a temperature of 400°F must be used, for although there is little danger of over-heating the wax to the point where it will burst into flames it is

These Scandinavian influenced candles add glamour to a special occasion

impossible to judge when the wax is at the correct temperature, and it is the temperature at which the wax is worked which gives many of the different effects.

Moulds. Although craft shops sell ready-made moulds of rubber, glass and metal, improvised moulds work very well and can produce fascinating shapes. Some household containers can be used, as long as they are leakproof and do not collapse under the heat of the wax. Yoghurt cartons, tins, cardboard cartons, plastic drainpipe, rubber balls, balloons, acetate and PVC sheeting are some of the things which can be utilized for moulds, but remember that the candle has to be removed when it has set, therefore the mould must either have a wide neck or be breakable.

Preparing the wax for coloured candles

Measure out the powdered wax or break up block wax into pieces. Measure out the stearin, one part stearin to ten parts of wax. Melt the stearin in a saucepan and then add the dye. Stir until all the particles of dye are dissolved. Melt the paraffin wax slowly in the second saucepan and then add the stearin and dye mixture.

White candles can be covered with a final layer of colour by dipping them into molten coloured wax. Float a 2 inch layer of molten coloured wax on hot water (heated at 82°C 180°F). Dip the white candle through the wax and into the water, then withdraw it so that it picks up colour along its length. If the wax is too hot very little colour will be picked up, and conversely, if the wax is too cool, the colour will be flaky. This dipping process can be repeated for depth of colour.

Candlemaking methods

Dipping

Dipping is one of the oldest methods of candlemaking and all that is required is wick, wax and an enamel jug, a little deeper than the required length of candle. Attach a piece of wick to a small stick. Fill the jug with wax heated at 82°C, 180°F. Dip the wick into the wax. Remove it and hold it in the air for about half a minute, or until the coat of wax has hardened. Dip again and repeat until the candle is thick enough. As the wax in the jug cools, bubbles will appear on the surface of the wax or the candle. When this happens, reheat the wax to 180°F. When the candle is finished, hang it to harden. For an all white candle or for one coloured throughout a good finishing shine can be given by giving a final dip

26

▲ *Statue-made mould* ▼ *Rolled beeswax sheets*

▲ *Ready made mould* ▼ *Carved dipped candle*

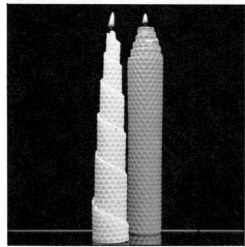

in wax heated to 200°F, 93°C, and then plunging the candle into cold water. If the jug is wide enough at the neck, several candles can be made by dipping simultaneously.

Ways with dipped candles

Moulding dipped candles

Candles can be moulded to shape by hand between dips. The pear shaped candles illustrated were made in this way.

Build up the candle to about ½ inch diameter, then start to dip or pour wax from half way up; the lower part of the candle will begin to thicken. At this stage, between dips, roll the candle between the hands towards the shape you want.

Carved candles

By dipping a short length of wick in a succession of different colours, building them up to about ¼ inch thick, multi-coloured layers are formed and these can be carved back with a sharp knife to great effect. For this process the wax must be very strongly dyed, or the layers of colour will show through each other.

To save wax follow the method given for floating coloured wax on hot water, but make a center core of at least 1 inch thickness by the normal dipping method first to prevent water getting on the wick.

Twist and plaits

A plait of three dipped candles in contrasting colours looks effective and these are easily made if someone else holds the ends while one plaits. A twisted candle is made with a finished but still soft dipped candle. Lay it on a smooth clean surface and flatten it gently with a rolling pin. Square off the base and, taking the candle in both hands, twist top and bottom in opposite directions. Cool immediately in cold water.

Beeswax candles

Sheets of pure beeswax, honeycomb textured and smelling delightfully of honey, can be used to make simple candles. These sheets are available from candlemakers suppliers. Choose a suitable wick and cut it to the desired candle length plus a few more inches. Lay the wick along one edge of the sheet and fold the wax over to cover

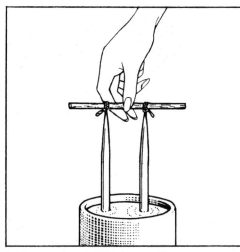

▲ *The technique of dipping candles*
▼ *The technique for layered candles*

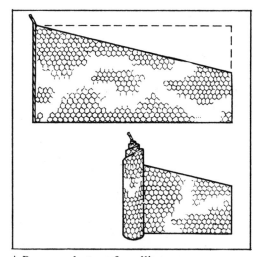

▲ *Beeswax sheet cut for rolling*
▼ *Candle mould suspended and filled*

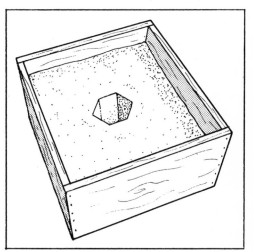

▲ *Damp sand prepared in a box*
▼ *The sand mould before carving*

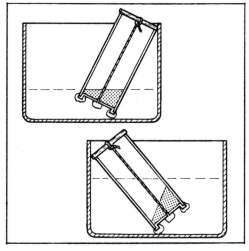

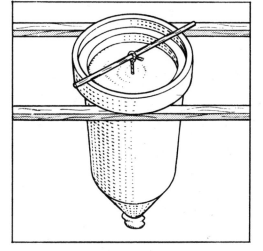

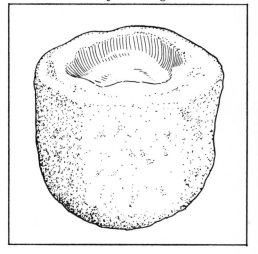

it. Roll up the candle, gently and evenly, making sure that the base is level. Trim the wick and dip it in molten beeswax. To make a pointed candle, cut the sheet of beeswax as shown in the diagram. Two contrasting tints of beeswax sheeting can be used together for variation.

Moulded candles

Ready-made moulds

Craft shops sell different kinds of ready-made candle moulds made of both metal and flexible latex rubber. Decorative relief candles are made in these in one casting. Treat latex rubber moulds with care, washing and drying them carefully after use. These moulds have no wick holes, and this has to be made with a wick needle. Make sure that the same hole is used each time the mould is used. To wick-up a mould thread the wick through, tyeing the bottom end to a rod or a stick with the top end of the wick pulled tight. Seal the hole with mould seal. Support the mould by hanging it on an improvised rack (see diagram).
To make a candle heat the wax to 180°F

and pour it slowly into the mould. Tap the sides of the mould gently to release air bubbles. After a short while a well will form round the wick as the cooling wax contracts. Prod the surface to break it and top up with wax heated to 180°F. Do this as often as necessary until the surface of the candle remains flat. If the candle seems to be misshapen, manipulate the mould with the hands while it is still soft. When the candle is completely cold and hardened rub the surface of the mould with soapy hands, and peel back the mould, taking care around the wick area. Return the mould to its original shape, wash and dry it. Remove the wick rod from the candle and trim the base.
The candle surface can be polished with hands or a soft cloth. Add a small amount of beeswax to the paraffin wax for a better shine.
Relief work can be highlighted by colouring the surface of the candle with water—soluble paint mixed with a little soap. Paint the candle and rub the colour off just before it dries, leaving some in the crevices. Do not over-do the colour because water soluble paint does not burn, and

may clog the wick if used to excess.

Making flexible moulds

Mould for making candles are made from a moulding liquid which is obtained from candle makers suppliers. Choose an ornament, jar or statue made from wood, glass, plastic, stone, plaster or clay. Make sure it is free from dust or grease.
Heat the object gently in front of a fire and dip it into the moulding liquid, covering it completely. Remove and hold the object until it stops dripping. The mould will set faster with a little heat, so hold the object in front of a fan heater until the whitish colour changes to yellow. The first few dips will go almost transparent. Air bubbles must be blown off and care must be taken not to touch the setting mould. Continue to dip until a smooth, even coat of about one sixteenth of an inch thick or more has built up. Leave the mould to stand until the moulding material has set. Trim uneven edges, and after rubbing the surface with liquid soap peel it away. Make a wick hole at the top of the mould and use it in exactly the same way as ready-made flexible moulds.

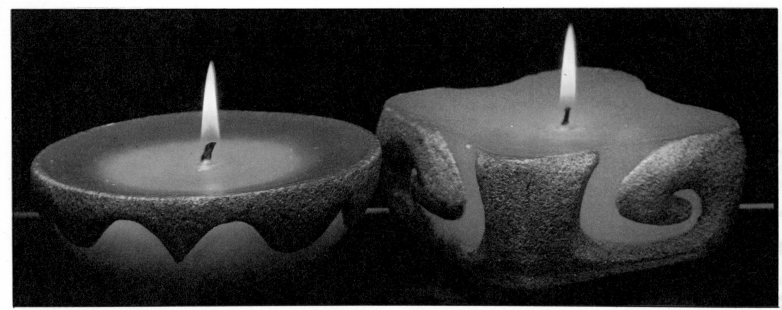

▲ Sand candles from an ashtray and bowl—carved into castles ▼   *▼ Two candles using the chunk technique. The square was made in a tea tin*

Other candlemaking techniques

Sand candles. Fill a box with damp sand and smooth off the surface without packing it down. Dig a hole out of the center and push an article into the hole to make a shaped hole.

An ashtray, small bowl or the end of a bottle will do. Heat the wax to 250°F, and pour it into shape in the sand, taking care to pour into the center of the hole. The hotter the wax, the more sand is picked up; at 250°F, between ½ inch and 1 inch is picked up. If a thicker sand wall is required, the wax should be hotter. Refill the hole as the level of the wax falls, keeping the temperature

of the wax high. Allow the sand candle to harden in a cold place for 1-2 hours. After this time, push the wicking needle down the center and leave it standing upright. Leave the candle overnight. Next day, dig the candle out, loosening the sand around it carefully and brushing away loose sand. Remove the needle and insert a wick which will leave an inch of wax unburned (for instance, if the candle is 3 inches in diameter put a 2 inch wick in). Top up with melted wax (220°F) and allow to set. Carve away areas of sand to make a design, taking care not to dig too deeply into the wax. If the right wick is chosen, the sand shell will remain intact after the candle has burned out and can be refilled.

Chunky candles. Arrange chunks of coloured wax in a mould, pressing them to the sides and keeping them as far apart as possible. Pour molten wax (200°F) over these chunks. Allow the mould to stand for one minute, then place in a cooling bath. Push a wicking needle down the center. When set, take the mould from the bath, and place it in water just under boiling point. The outside of the wax will melt, and the coloured chunks will also melt and blend with the new wax. Top up with wax at 180°F, covering the whole surface of the candle and allowing the wax to flow down the inside of the mould so that the whole surface is covered with molten wax. Place mould in a cooling bath again and allow to harden. Remove

28

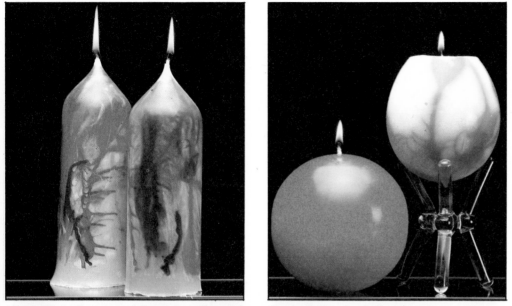

▲▼ *Marbled effects on multilayered candles, and two from a ball and a balloon* ▲

▲▼ *Beeswax candles and water candles*

candle, put in wick.

Marbled candles. Fix a wick in a warmed solid mould, and pour in a wax-stearin mixture at 190°F. Allow a minute for air bubbles to rise, then place in a cooling ·bath for 40 seconds. Pour the unset wax back into the pan, leaving a wax shell in the mould. Then, using pure dye, spoon a little into the mould, and quickly swirl it round and tip away the excess. Do this two or three times· with different colours until a design has built up. Then pour in half a cup of candle wax (180°F), swirl it round quickly and empty the excess into a separate container (so that the wax will not contaminate white wax if it has picked up colour). Do this seven or eight times to trap the colour between

two layers of white wax. Then fill the mould with candle wax in the usual way. To achieve a well defined pattern it is essential that the mould is kept warm and that there is no waiting between processes.

Multi-layered candles. These are made by pouring different coloured waxes into a mould at 82°F, allowing each layer to partially set before adding the next colour. By standing the mould at an angle in a cooling bath, layers can be built up diagonally.

Ball candles. Round candles are made using a rubber ball as a mould. Cut the ball in half and cut a hole in the top. Stick the two halves together again with sticky tape.

Whipped cream candles. Whip cooling

wax with a fork to make a frothy mixture and use it to make candles in moulds which wouldn't stand higher temperatures.

Water candles. These strange looking candles are intended to be used for table decorations but they can be burned. Put a small quantity of melted wax (210°F) into a saucer and, wearing rubber gloves, hold a plain candle upright, resting in the wax. Holding the saucer in one hand and the candle in the other, push the candle and saucer into a bucket of cold water with a swift, smooth movement. The wax will float upwards, and practice will gradually make the formation less random. By twisting the saucer as it is immersed, the wax can be swirled around the candle.

Daisy patterns

You would be surprised what you can make from a daisy and how easy they are to do! Once you have tried daisy work, you won't be able to put it down—nor will the children. It is so quick you can make dozens of them in an evening while watching television or whiling away a long journey. Two daisies make a pair of earrings, six a headband or choker, twelve add up to a doll's dress, sixteen an unusual belt. And if you keep going, you can soon make enough for a poncho, shawl, or even a long skirt. This chapter covers making separate flowers, while later chapters tell you how to sew and crochet them together and how to fill the center to make very decorative daisies.

Daisies in the making

Daisies can be made from whatever you like, usually wool or thick cotton yarns—or even string, lurex or raffia. Daisies can be washed, but are impossible to iron without flattening. So either choose a bulky man-made yarn which will spring back into shape after washing or be prepared for dry-cleaning.

Most needlework departments stock the Hero Crazy Daisy Winder in 2 inch and 3 inch diameters. To make your own, or to make larger or smaller daisies, simply stick ordinary straight pins around a ring of thick cardboard and pull out the pins when the daisy is completely finished.

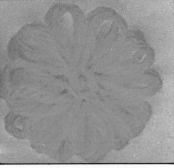

Separate daisies

With manufactured daisy makers you will see from the directions that you have to turn the knob to push out the spokes. Hold the daisy maker in the left hand with the flat side facing you. If you are making your own, insert 12 pins around a circle of cardboard 2 inches in diameter.

Hold the end of yarn down with the left thumb. Then, working in a clockwise direction, pass

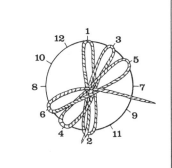

yarn with the right hand from left to right around spoke 1, pass yarn across center and

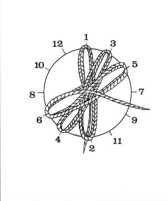

from right to left around spoke 2 opposite, back across center; from left to right around spoke 3, and right to left around spoke 4. Continue until all spokes have been wrapped (once if using thick yarn, several times for thinner yarn) and cut, leaving a tail about 12 inches long.

Closed centers

For a one-colour daisy, thread needle with the tail of yarn. Work 13 back stitches, passing needle under 2 petals and back over 1. Make sure to do all 13 back stitches or the center will not be complete. Work in the

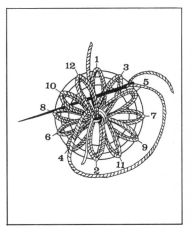

starting end with weaving stitches to bind it firmly, and fasten both yarns on the top side of the daisy (this will be the back when the daisy is finished). Pull in the spokes or pull out your pins, and the daisy is complete.

To make a daisy with a center in a contrasting colour, take a second yarn, secure it to the center of the daisy with two or three back stitches and continue as before, remembering to bind in both ends of the first colour.

Daisy trimmings

Use separate daisies as a trimming — they look so sweet scattered on the little girl's party dress shown opposite. For a twelve year old party-goer, trim the yoke of a plain navy or red dress with white

daisies or scatter them around the hem. For a winter bride make a full-length creamy wool dress with long belled sleeves and decorate the sleeves in matching daisies of wool yarn with pearls sewn to the centers.

Joining daisies

Once you have discovered how to make daisies with closed centers (see previous page) you can begin to be more ambitious. The daisies can be worked with open centers which in themselves can be decorated with beads.

The edges of the daisies, too, lend themselves to decoration although it is not essential to edge single daisies, especially if you like a random petal effect. The lock stitch edging shown in this chapter makes for a neater and more stylised finish which holds the petals firmly in their original shape and if you want to make your daisies into a trimming this edging is part of the basic method.

Open centers

Thread needle with tail of yarn. Put needle into center of daisy and pull it through between any two petals. Put needle into center again and bring it out between the next two petals, working clockwise. Continue overcasting, working an extra (13th) stitch to make the center complete. Finish off by threading the needle through the loop of the 13th stitch before pulling it tight. Then thread the needle under the overcasting to hide the knot.

Decorative centers

There's no end to the ways you can decorate daisies. Add a pearl or rhinestone to the center for evening daisies or coloured wooden or glass beads, buttons (the smooth, rounded ones which have a shank at the back for sewing to the fabric) or even sunflower seeds. When you finish overcasting, push the needle up through the center, thread it through the pearl or rhinestone then sew through the opposite side of the hole. Make another overcasting stitch there to secure the bead then draw the needle through the loop of the next stitch and finish off as for the open center daisy.

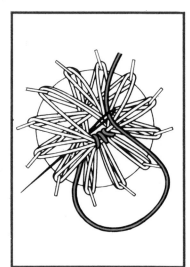

Overcasting an open center

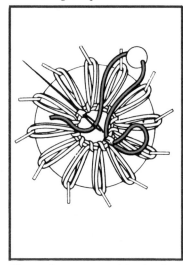

Decorating a center with a bead

Lock stitch edging

1. Make a daisy in the usual way but leave a tail 14 inches long when you begin. Then, keeping the daisy on the daisy maker, thread up with the tail of wool. Take the needle upwards through the center of a petal to the left of the spoke. Thread the needle through again, to the right of the spoke, leaving a loop.

2. Thread needle through this loop from right to left and pull tight with a gentle jerk so that the knot locks below the spoke. Stitch each petal in turn in the same way, leaving a fairly loose thread between each spoke. When circle is complete, take end of thread back to the center and finish off. Release the daisy from the daisy maker.

To join daisies

3. Make one daisy complete with lock stitch edging. Make a second, without the edging, and leave it on the daisy maker. Taking the completed daisy, place it wrong side up to cover the daisy on the daisy maker. Begin the lock stitch edging, going through two petals only of both top and bottom daisy.

4. Turn back the top daisy and finish edging the bottom daisy as described in **2.**

To make a pretty trimming or edging for a dress make and join together in the way just described as many daisies as you require.

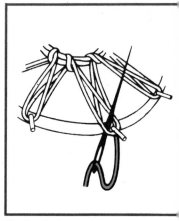

Lock stitch: step 1

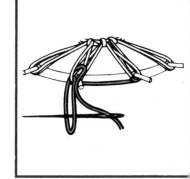

Lock stitch: step 2

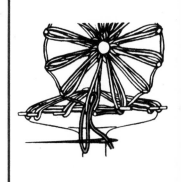

Joining two daisies

Working a chain of daisies

Square daisies

Place adapter on the Knit-Wit. Wind wool across adapter from daisy to daisy following instructions for round daisy. However, wool will lie across opening of each post. Make two windings, overcast stitches in center, and lock-stitch edging according to instructions for round daisy.

NB After releasing, square may appear to be cup-shaped. Take square in both hands and stretch gently to bring corners out to true square shape

Joining square daisies

When joining square daisies, work same as for round daisy except that you join 4 petals of top square to 4 petals of bottom square by starting joining at one post of adapter, working following two spokes, finishing joining at 2nd post of adapter (one complete side of square).

Square daisy on adapter

Daisy babies

Making a crib blanket is a perfect way to start joining square daisies. It's small enough for individual daisies to retain their importance, is quick to finish and lends itself to pretty decoration. Here the centers of some of the daisies have been embroidered to emphasize their 'daisy-ness', but you could apply a few separate daisies instead, or attach a pompon to each corner, or make each in a different colour for a patchwork effect.

You will need: 6oz Bernat Berella Baby Bulky yarn and 1oz of contrast yarn (100% orlon for washability). Knit-Wit.

The blanket consists of eleven rows of fifteen square daisies. Follow the instructions for making and joining these on the previous page. When the first row is completed, add each new individual daisy by working lock stitch edging to form the next row and by joining each addition to the previous row as well as to one another. Oversew the centers of the daisies around the edge with contrast yarn and also decorate a ring of centers down the middle.

3D effects for a beautiful bedspread

Three-dimensional daisies give an unusual effect for an afghan or bedspread. Quick and easy to do, it is great fun and is something which can be tackled by all the family.

The Multi-fleur daisy loom is different from the other looms so far mentioned in previous daisy work chapters. The loom consists of a plastic ring with fixed pegs set at right angles. There is an inner circle and an outer circle of pegs so that daisies of different sizes can be worked, or three-dimensional daisies with different sized petals. Each daisy measures about 3¼ inches and, with 2 ounces of colour A and 1 ounce each of colours B and C in double knitting wool, about 32 daisies can be made working the full loom.

When using different yarns, calculate the amount needed by the yardage. Allowing for different tensions, each daisy takes about 4 yards colour A (outer petals), 2¼ yards colour B (inner petals) and 2 yards colour C (joining chain).

How to wind the daisy

Work with the loom on a flat surface and space 1 at the top. Start with the large outer petals. Place the end of the yarn in space 7 and fasten with sticky tape. Take yarn across to space 1, around outer peg to space 12, back across to space 6, around outer peg to space 7 (see diagram **1**). Wind yarn around same pegs twice more so that each petal has 3 loops.

Continuing with the strand at space 7, take it across to space 2 (diagram **2**), around outer peg to space 1, across to space 7, around outer peg to space 8 (diagram **3**). Wind yarn around same pegs twice more to complete petals.

Continue in this way in an anti-clockwise direction until all pegs have been used and there are 12 3-loop petals, ending with yarn in space 6. Cut about ½-inch of yarn beyond the loom and secure with sticky tape.

Using the B colour, secure end of yarn at space 7, take it across to space 1, around inner peg to space 12, across to space 6, around inner peg to space 7. Wind yarn around same pegs once more so that each petal has 2 loops.

Continuing with yarn at space 7, take it across to space 2, around inner peg to space 1 (diagram **4**), across to space 7, around inner peg to space 8. Wind yarn around same pegs once more to complete petals.

Continue in this way to wind the inner pegs until there are 12 2-loop petals, ending with yarn in space 6. Cut yarn leaving about 16 inches for sewing. Thread the end into a darning needle, pass around the inner peg to space 7 and push needle through to the back at center, taking care not to split the yarn (diagram **5**). Finish off by bringing needle up through space 12, pull tightly against center back of flower, push needle through to back between strands in space 1. Continue this backstitch until every petal has a crossbar, keeping the stitch as firm and near the center as possible. End with the yarn at the back of the loom in space 10. Push

▲ *Six stages of winding a daisy on to the Multi-Fleur loom*

the needle through from back to front at center and then from front to back at inner edge of any backstitch (diagram **6**). Gently remove flower from loom and fasten the end securely on the wrong side. Trim the loose ends close to the center of the flower.

Joining the daisies

With the method of joining illustrated (see diagram) the daisies retain their circular shape rather than making them into squares (Daisy work chapter 3) or joining in each daisy as it is worked (Daisy work chapter 2). This is an ideal method for a wide variety of pretty things. Begin with a small project such as a baby's bonnet or a pretty evening shawl with matching handbag.

1st row With crochet hook No.F and colour C, make loop on hook. Working from right side of flower, work 1sc in any outer petal of a flower, taking all 3 loops with care not to twist them. * Ch5, 1sc in next petal, repeat from * 6 times more, leaving last 4 petals free. ***Skipping 5ch, work 1sc in any petal on a new flower, ch5, 1sc in next petal on new flower, drop loop from hook, insert hook in sc of 7th petal of previous flower and then in dropped loop of new flower, draw this loop through sc. ** Ch5, 1sc in next petal of new flower, repeat from ** 5 times more, leaving last 4 petals free. Repeat from *** as desired.

Continue across free petals of first row as follows: from right side, ch5, 1sc in 9th petal of last flower, * ch5, 1sc in next petal, repeat

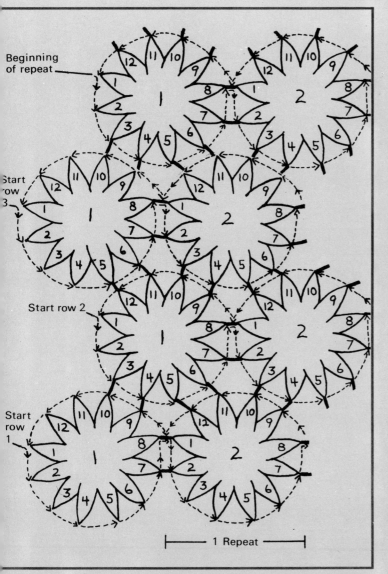

Follow the arrows on this chart for the method of joining the daisies

▲ *Detail of the daisy afghan shown here as a bedspread*

from * twice more. *** 5ch, 1dc in joining between last and next flower, 5ch, 1dc in 9th petal of next flower, ** 5ch, 1dc in next petal, repeat from ** twice more. Repeat from *** across all free petals ending with 5ch, join with ss in first dc. Fasten off.

NB Rows are always worked from left to right.

2nd row 1dc in any petal of a new flower, 5ch, 1dc in 2nd petal, 5ch, 1dc in 3rd petal, drop loop from hook, insert hook in dc on 10th petal of first flower of previous row and then in dropped loop, draw this loop through dc, 5ch, 1dc in 4th petal of new flower, join to next petal of first flower of previous row as before, 5ch, 1dc in 5th petal of new flower, join to 12th petal of 2nd flower of previous row, 5ch, 1dc in 6th petal of new flower, join to dc on next petal of 2nd flower of previous row, 5ch, 1dc in 7th petal of new flower, 5ch, 1dc in 8th petal of new flower, leaving last 4 petals free. ***Omitting 5ch, work 1dc in any petal of a new flower, 5ch, 1dc in 2nd petal of new flower, join to 7th petal of last flower, 5ch, 1dc in 3rd petal of new flower, join to next free petal in previous row, 5ch, 1dc in 4th petal of new flower, join to next free petal in previous row, 5ch, 1dc in 5th petal of new flower, join to next free petal of next flower in previous row, 5ch, 1dc in 6th petal of new flower, join to next free petal in previous row, 5ch, 1dc in 7th petal of new flower, 5ch, 1dc in 8th petal of new flower leaving last 4 petals free. Repeat from *** as required. Continue across free petals as for 1st row.

3rd row 1dc in any petal of a new flower, * 5ch, 1dc in next petal, repeat from * 3 times more, join to dc on 12th petal of first flower of previous row, 5ch, 1dc in 6th petal of new flower, join to next petal in previous row, 5ch, 1dc in 7th petal of new flower, 5ch, 1dc in 8th petal of new flower, leaving last 4 petals free. Repeat from 2nd row *** to second last flower, omitting 5ch, work 1dc in any petal of a new flower, 5ch, 1dc in 2nd petal of new flower, join to 7th petal of last flower, 5ch, 1dc in 3rd petal of new flower, join to next free petal in previous row, 5ch, 1dc in 4th petal of new flower, join to next free petal in previous row, * 5ch, 1dc in next petal of new flower, repeat from * 3 times more, ending with dc in 8th petal, leaving last 4 petals free. Continue across free petals as given for 1st row.

Repeat 2nd and 3rd rows as required.

Fasten ends securely.

To make an afghan

An afghan can be used as a rug or a bedspread. To make one measuring about 48in by 62in you will need 357 daisies. This will take 22 1oz balls colour A (illustrated here in white), 13 1oz balls colour B (yellow) and 10 1oz balls colour C (green), all in double knitting. Join the daisies in alternating rows of 16 and 15 to make 23 rows in all. When completed, pin out with rust proof pins and cover with a damp cloth. Do not remove pins until cloth is dry.

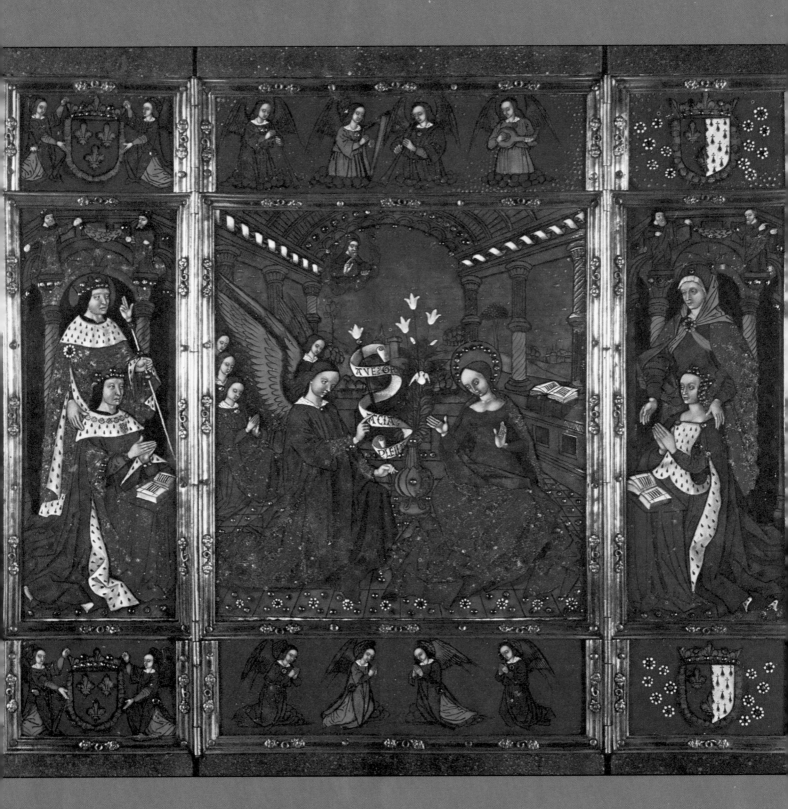

Enamelling

The art of enamelling has been practiced for at least two thousand years and may have originated in Western Europe: early Greek writers describe the colourful designs of the enamel-decorated weapons and armour used by northern barbarians. In early examples of Greek and Celtic enamel work only opaque enamels were used, and it was not until the 12th century that glowing, translucent colours appeared in the work of the Gothic enamellers. The craft gradually developed, and fine examples were produced by the jewellers of Elizabethan England and in France in the 18th century. By the early 20th century, the enamellers of the Russian firm of Carl Faberge were producing work of incredible precision and technique. In recent years, the art of enamelling has enjoyed a revival, and artists are again using techniques which have not changed, basically, for many hundreds of years.

The word 'enamel' is sometimes used to describe a substance such as paint or varnish applied to glaze a surface. Enamelling, in the context used here, is a technique whereby a kind of glass ground to a powder, and coloured by the addition of metal oxides, is fused by heat to a metal surface. Copper, silver and gold are the metals most commonly used with glass powder enamel, and of these copper has the advantage of being inexpensive, of standing up to fairly rough treatment, and of having a high melting point. Silver gives a greater degree of reflection and is most suitable for the transparent green and blue enamels. Gold is the supreme metal for enamelling, and is particularly suitable as a background for transparent red colours, although its price puts it beyond reach of most amateur enamellers.

This triptych of Limoges enamelled panels shows the craft at its most exquisite

The techniques of enamelling

The five basic enamelling techniques in use are still known by their French names, and date from the 11th or 12th centuries. These are Limoges, Cloisonne, Champleve, Basse-Taille, and Plique à jour.

Cloisonne is thought to be the oldest technique. The name comes from the word 'cloison' meaning enclosure, and in this work narrow wires are soldered on to a base plate in a pattern, with the spaces in between filled with the enamel, which is usually opaque.

In Champleve enamelling (the word means 'raised field') hollows are carved out of the metal and are then filled with enamel. This is somewhat similar to Basse-Taille (meaning 'low-cut'), a more advanced form of Champleve in which the recesses are also decorated with low relief carving which shows through the transparent enamels used in this process.

Transparent enamels are also used in Plique à jour ('light of day') which produces an effect similar to that of a stained glass window.

These processes all involve filling recesses with enamel, but the Limoges technique, named after the town in France where it originated, does not rely on metal carving or Cloisons, and is therefore the most suitable for the beginner.

Equipment and materials

It is usually supposed that enamelling is a process involving high temperature firing and quantities of expensive equipment, and is therefore unsuitable for the amateur. This is not entirely true. It is possible to produce enamelled pieces suitable for jewellery using a small kiln, or even a Bunsen burner or a gas torch. In some circumstances it is even possible to fire pieces on a gas or electric cooker.

Enamel powders and copper shapes are obtained from specialist suppliers. The only other equipment necessary for the craft are shaker boxes or sieves made from wire mesh (80 or 60 mesh) used for sprinkling the enamel powders. A mesh bottomed tea or coffee strainer makes a good shaker, and this gives a good idea of the coarseness of the material needed if you decide to make your own. Match box trays with the base removed and replaced with a small piece of cotton organdie make effective shakers. Some enamels come in glass jars with a sieve lid, which saves using a shaker.

A spatula or palette knife is useful for placing pieces in and removing pieces from the kiln or flame, but an old kitchen knife will do just as well, if it is flexible.

◄ *The pendant worn with a matching bracelet*

Making a simple pendant

This piece is made by the Limoges method, in which the entire surface area of the metal is covered with enamel. The enamels can be applied by dusting, painting or stencilling, and chunks of enamel or glass beads can be introduced to vary the surface structure. The method for a simple dusting and painting technique is given here.

You will need

A small enamelling kiln (or an improvised firing arrangement, such as a Bunsen burner under a piece of wire mesh on a tripod stand).
Copper shapes, either pre-formed or cut from 18 gauge copper (No.2).
Enamel in powder form (two colours).
Two shaker boxes.
Spatula or palette knife.
Sheets of paper.
Light machine oil (sewing machine oil) or glycerine.
Brushes (No.1 or 2) and steel pen nibs in holders.
Fine steel wool.
Vinegar.
Leather thong.

Stage 1. Prepare the copper shape by filing and smoothing the edges and cleaning the entire surface of the shape with fine steel wool, so that the enamel will fuse with the metal.
Immerse the copper in vinegar and leave for a minute or two, then wash in water and dry. This will remove any grease or dirt. After cleaning, the copper should be handled only by the edges. The point to remember is that the copper has to be clean and grease-free to allow the enamel to fuse properly.

Stage 2. Lay the prepared copper shape on a clean piece of paper, with a coin to prop it up at one corner so that the spatula can be inserted easily underneath. Using the shaker box, dust the enamel powder over the whole surface of the metal until an even coating of enamel powder covers the copper shape.

Stage 3. Lift the sprinkled piece with the spatula or knife, and place it in the kiln. The excess enamel powder which has fallen on the sheet of paper can be replaced in the shaker.

Stage 4. It is now time to turn on the heat. Follow the manufacturer's instructions for heating the kiln. If a Bunsen burner is being used, turn it on fully to get as much heat as possible, and place the flame directly under the piece to be fired. During firing, which takes two or three minutes, the enamel will at first

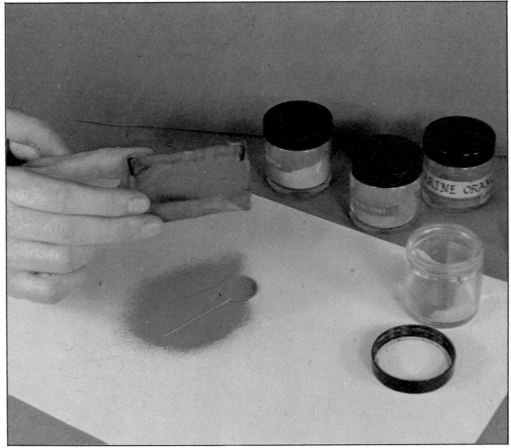

▲ Stage 2 of the process, where the first colour is sifted over the copper shape
▼ Once an even coating of powder has been applied, lift the piece with a spatula

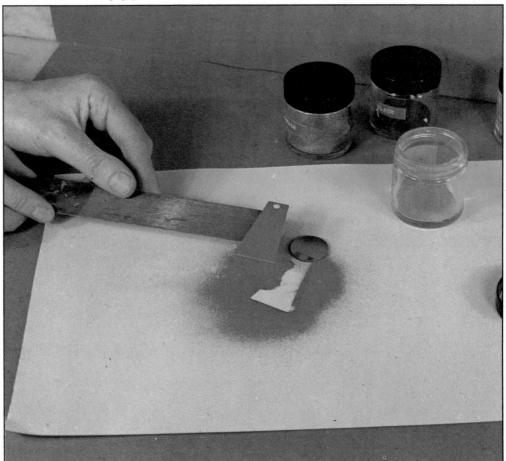

appear to discolour, and will then glisten as it begins to melt and fuse with the copper. If a closed kiln is used, and there is no observation hole, it is possible to open the door slightly and check the visual appearance of the work. But this must be done carefully in order not to lose too much heat.

When an even, glassy appearance can be seen, the heat is turned off and the piece allowed to cool.

Stage 5. Having achieved a nice, evenly coloured surface on the shape you can now add a second dusting of colour to create a decorative pattern. During the second dusting it is important to ensure that no fire scale from the back of the copper shape becomes mixed with the enamel, as this would spoil it for future use. To avoid this possibility clean the back of the piece after the first firing with steel wool, or else apply a saline solution to the back beforehand which will facilitate the removal of fire scale. One tablespoonful of salt to a cup of water makes a suitable solution. Apply it with a brush. Follow this procedure between each firing.

Either glycerine or a light oil are used as adhesives for the second and subsequent colours. Having pre-planned a design draw it on the clean enamel surface in oil or glycerine using either a pen or fine brush.

A second dusting of enamel powder in a contrasting colour is then applied from a shaker and will adhere to the oil drawing. Any excess powder is removed by tapping the piece on its end.

When the second dusting has been completed, return the piece to the kiln for refiring.

The second colour will melt and fuse with the first layer which will also remelt, and the process is complete when an even, glassy finish is obtained.

Stage 6. Allow the piece to cool, then clean the edges and back with steel wool and metal polish. Take care when cleaning the edges to rub away from the enamel surface to avoid chipping the actual edge. Complete the pendant by adding a leather thong and perhaps giving the back a coat of metal lacquer.

This pendant uses only two colours, but others can be added by the same method, cleaning off between firings.

Experiment with different finishes and effects by dusting the second colour through a paper stencil or by sifting the powder all over the first firing and then scratching a design with the end of a matchstick. Once the technique has been mastered and you are happy with the results, you can progress to larger and more involved pieces of work.

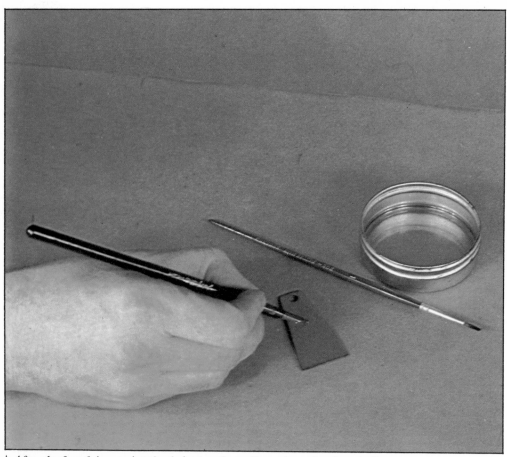

▲ *After the first firing, paint the design on the surface using a brush and oil*
▼ *Stage 5, with the second colour powder adhering to the oil-painted design ready for second firing*

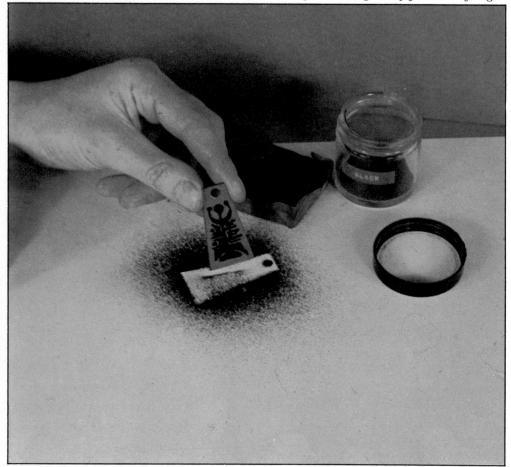

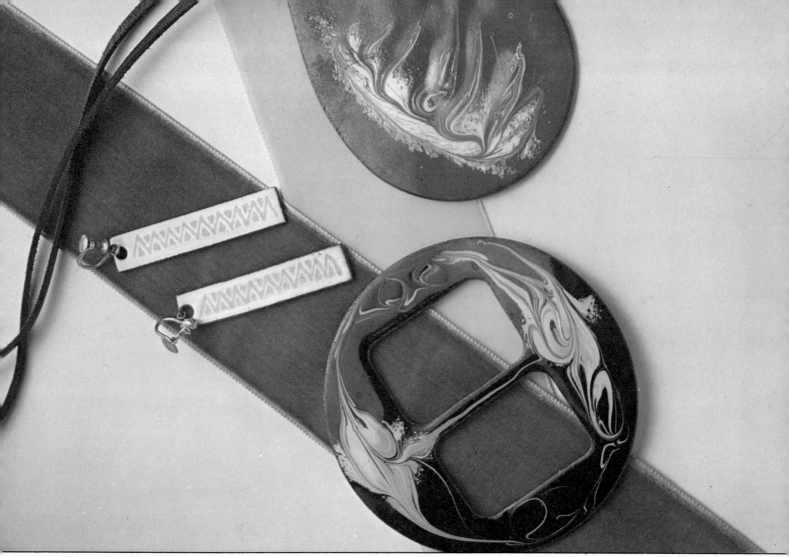

▲ The buckle is the result of two firings, one black, the second yellow and green ▼ The oblong pendant in this picture is an example of the Cloisonne technique

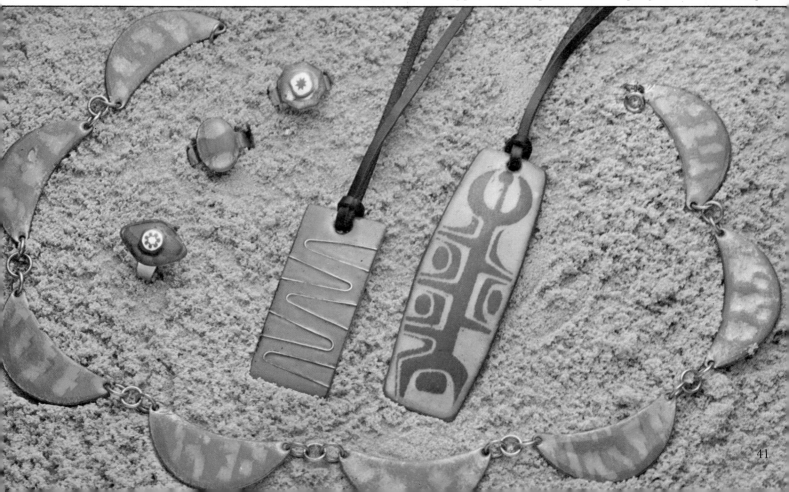

Fabric boxes

The forgotten craft

Making embroidered fabric boxes is in some ways a forgotten craft. Many people, keen embroiderers, never think of turning their stitchcraft into the production of boxes—yet an exquisitely made fabric box provides the maker with a tremendous sense of achievement. Embroidered fabric boxes make marvellous gifts—but having made one you'll find it difficult to part with it.

Boxes take time, patience and care to make and measurements must be absolutely accurate if they are to look professional. Cleanliness is essential for this craft.

Work with a clean cloth over your lap, and wash the hands frequently while working. Remember that adhesive dropped onto fabric will often leave a permanent mark and vigilance is needed during the glueing stages.

Materials and equipment

Boxes are made of cardboard which is then padded and covered with fabric. Various weights of card are used in box making and each of the projects in this chapter recommend the most suitable weight of card. Fabric adhesive is used for all glueing and it is best to use a

narrow spatula for applying it.

Equipment needed for this craft is little more than you would need for any sewing craft, but you will also need a steel ruler, a good quality cutting knife, a square and a piece of hardboard for cutting on.

Fabrics and padding

Thin smooth fabrics are better than thick ones, and those without excessive stretch in them are best. Silk, satin, rayon, linen, cotton, velvet and felt are all suitable fabrics, and those with lurex finishes or rich-looking prints make superb

This beautiful box is encrusted with beads and embroidery and depicts the life and wealth of its owners in detail

▲ *Make large boxes for sewing materials, jewellery, keepsakes; small boxes for pins and rings. Vary the fabric and decoration to suit yourself*

jewel boxes. The top of the box can be left plain if desired, or can be decorated with appliqué, beadwork, goldwork or surface embroidery of almost any kind to produce the desired effect.

Initials make boxes individual and beads can be piled one on another with sequins added for a jewelled effect. All surface embroidery must be completed before starting to construct the box. If patterned fabrics are used, boxes often look prettier unadorned.

Padding materials

The padding of the boxes which is placed immediately under the top fabric should be a plain fabric, Pellon is usually recommended.

Planning a box

Draw out the box you intend to make first of all as a rough perspective drawing (diagram 1), and then draw out each piece, marking the measurements. Lining pieces are made smaller because one must allow

for the thickness of padding and the covering material. Tremendous care must be taken in these measurements if lids are to fit properly and not be too loose or fall into the edges of the box.

As you cut out each piece of card, mark it clearly on the wrong side for outer, and right side for linings, so that you know which part of the box it is and whether it is a lining piece or outer piece. The mark is made because you will be covering one side of the card with fabric, and pieces can

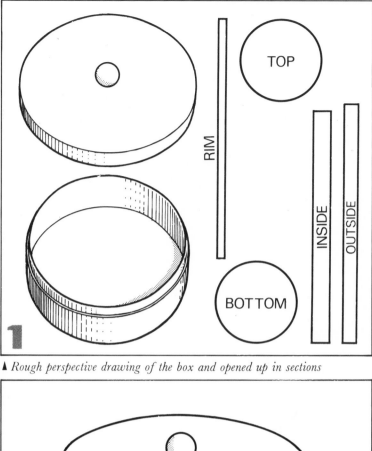

1

▲ *Rough perspective drawing of the box and opened up in sections*

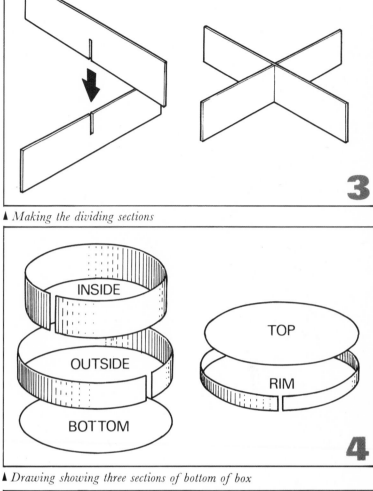

3

▲ *Making the dividing sections*

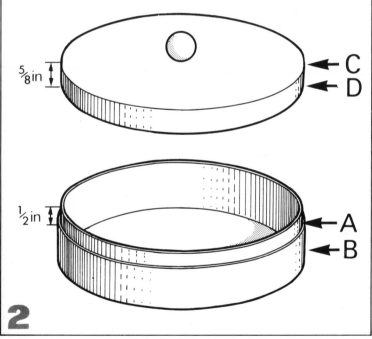

2

▲ *The various parts marked A, B, C, D*

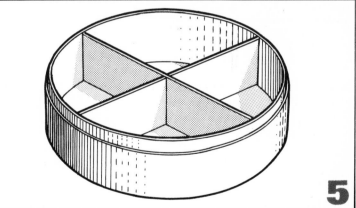

4

▲ *Drawing showing three sections of bottom of box*

5

▲ *Showing sections in place*

easily lose their identity and become a bewildering muddle once you have begun to cover and pad.

Round box with overlapping lid

Ticket card is used for the sides and the lining of the box. Four-sheet card is used for the top and base. The outside measurement is just over 3 times (3·14) the diameter of the box bottom.

Method

Cut the lining card for the inside (marked A on diagram 1) so that it makes a circle ½ inch deeper than the outer box side (marked B on diagram 2).

From both sections, cut lining and outer into circles, butting the ends and sticking the join with sticky tape (do not overlap joins because this causes a bump). Remember that when these two circles are fitted inside one another the joins must be kept apart or they form an ugly bump.

Top

Cut out a circle from the four-sheet card for the outside of the lid (C diagram 2). This should be exactly the diameter of the outside circle (B) just formed. Cut out the lining for the lid from the ticket card, making it slightly smaller than the outside lid.

Rim of lid

Cut this in ticket card so that it makes a circle exactly the same circumference as

▲ *Carefully thought-out abstract designs, worked in beads, sequins and thread on a plain fabric, can make an unusual decoration for a box lid*

▼ *Open Cretan stitch, used to stitch together sections of fabric*   ▼ *Mitring and snipping for lining and covering fabrics*

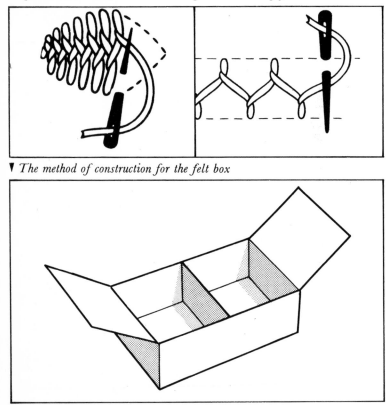

▼ *The method of construction for the felt box*

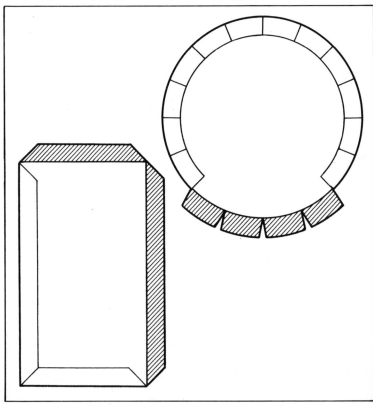

▲ *Richly embroidered fabrics, although expensive, make beautiful boxes. A small piece can be used to cover a little box for rings and brooches*

the lid, and $\frac{5}{8}$ inch deep (D, diagram 2). Butt and join into a circle and stick with sticky tape.

Bottom

Cut four-sheet card to exactly the same diameter circle as the top and then cut the lining slightly smaller.

Cutting the fabric

Cut fabrics for both outside of box and lining to the above sizes, allowing $\frac{1}{2}$ inch turnings. Allow a $\frac{3}{4}$ inch extra when cutting the lining for (A) as it has to turn over the lip. Allow extra when cutting fabric for D as it has to turn under the rim.

Padding

Padding is cut to the same size as the card.

Applying padding

Padding sides of box. Glue two thicknesses of padding to the inside of the lining card and to the outside of the outer card, butting joins.

Padding the bottom. Cut two pieces of padding to the exact size of the bottom and two more pieces $\frac{1}{2}$ inch larger all round. Using one same size and one larger size, glue the two thicknesses to the outside of the outer card and two thicknesses to the inside of the lining card. The bigger piece of padding is brought over the card edge to round it off. Snip the edges for a smooth finish and glue down.

Padding the top. Glue two thicknesses of padding to the inside of the lining card and at least three thicknesses of padding to the outside of the lid piece (C).

Stages of covering the box

Covering the sections. 1. Join the side pieces of both outer and lining fabrics into a circle and press seams flat (A and B pieces).

2. Join rim fabric into a circle and press. Cover the side pieces A and B with fabric, glueing it into position and when completely dry, slip piece A into piece B.

3. Cover rim piece D with fabric over sewing the open, upper edges together.

4. Cover the outside of the bottom circle and the inside of the lining circle with fabric, taking turnings over the edges.

5. Cover the top circle with fabric and decide at this point if a knob or top decoration is required. If so, stitch the knob to the circle, stitching right through the card.

6. Stitch the rim to the top (along oversewn edge of rim) using open Cretan stitch and six strands of thread.

7. Join bottom circle to sides, using open Cretan stitch. When stitching pieces together, stitches should go through fabric and padding but not through the card. Keep stitches regularly spaced.

8. Decide at this point if box divisions are required (see diagram 3). Cover card without padding it and then stitch the divisions to the bottom lining circle.

9. Put adhesive on the inside of the bottom circle and carefully press the lining section down upon it.

Put adhesive on the inside of the lid and press lining section onto it.

Leave to dry.

Square boxes

Square boxes are made in exactly the same way as round boxes except that the four pieces of the lip and rim are sewn together at the joins.

Fabric collage

The word collage is derived from the French phrase 'papier collé', or pasted paper, and means, literally, the art of sticking pieces of paper, sticks, wood, and fabric onto a background to make a picture.

In fabric collage, although the picture is mainly composed of material, other things such as beads, lace, shells, feathers or braids can be introduced to give texture, and sometimes a few stitches are added for decoration or to hold down a piece of fabric. The art of making fabric pictures is a long established one, but because present day adhesives have more reliability and are easier to use the art of fabric collage has, on the whole, developed fairly recently.

There are one or two charming examples in museums dating from the late nineteenth century, made chiefly of paper with figures dressed in fabric, and these show that the interest has always been there, if not the technique.

This detail is from a modern collage that depicts life in the small Oxfordshire village of Charlbury

49

Designs for collage

Almost any pictorial-type design can be turned into collage, and for a beginner children's books will provide some delightful illustrations for inspiration. Make sketches of scenes which appeal to you and keep a scrapbook of cuttings collected from magazines and newspapers. Poems, music, and television programmes can all be sources of inspiration for picture making, and so are the shapes and colours of nature. Look carefully at a bunch of flowers or an old stone wall—they will give you lovely ideas for colour schemes which can be incorporated into your work. Look again at a favourite painting, and see how the artist had used colour to interpret his ideas in fabric. Museums and art galleries will also give you a wealth of ideas for collage pictures, and you can buy postcard reproductions of works of art which can be taken home and studied at leisure. Animals, birds, flowers, fruit, fish, the countryside, the market place, children, the kitchen, your garden—inspiration for collage is all around you, for the taking.

▲▼ Swan queen collage with printed silk background, the swan worked in metallic fabrics and padded

Equipment and materials for collage

You will need:

- [ ] Scissors for cutting fabric and paper, large for general cutting, small for fine work (it's best to have more than one pair of each, so that if one gets lost among the fabrics, another is at hand)
- [ ] Scrap paper, for roughing out designs
- [ ] Pencil
- [ ] Pins and needles
- [ ] Adhesives suitable for fabric work (ie latex adhesives)
- [ ] Spreader for use with adhesives and some cocktail sticks
- [ ] Sewing thread, wools and silks for the odd stitching required
- [ ] Iron and ironing board
- [ ] Strong, firm fabrics for backing, such as Pellon, paper-backed burlap, felt, cotton, mattress ticking.
- [ ] White cardboard for mounting (not brown, it may discolour fabrics)
- [ ] Tweezers to grasp delicate bits of fabric
- [ ] A weight of some sort to hold materials in place while the adhesive sets, such as a felt covered brick
- [ ] Set square and ruler

Fabrics

These are the raw material of collage and from them ideas will grow for pictures. Save scraps from dressmaking, no matter how small, and beg them from friends. Go to jumble sales and buy old clothes. Don't part readily with old dresses. If you can persuade a shopkeeper to let you

have them, pattern books and sample swatches will provide a wide selection of colours and textures. Felt is useful because it doesn't fray, and it is dense enough to prevent adhesive seeping through.

Nets will come in handy for misty, romantic effects. Small bits of fur fabric are invaluable for animal pictures. Gold and silver Lurex fabrics will add a touch of luxury and splendour. Dull-surfaced fabrics will also be needed to offset bright ones, so keep some of those in your bits bag and some strong firmly textured fabrics for backgrounds. Patterned fabrics which will suggest forms and shapes for pictures are invaluable—corduroy for ploughed fields, green chenille for trees, black lace for wrought iron, red and white striped cotton for awnings, and so on. Textures can be as important as colours in fabric collage, so look for tweeds and other knobbly materials, and shiny, sleek and velvety surfaces. Raffia, Lurex yarn, fringes, ribbons, lace, bits of crochet work, string, beads, cotton wool, cords, silks, wools, feathers, braids, sequins, buttons— all of these should be saved and kept for collage.

Storing materials

You need to keep your bits and pieces in some sort of order, otherwise you will never be able to find anything when you need it.

Large transparent polythene bags are one of the best ways of storing materials. Either store them in bags by colour, or, if you prefer it, in textures, thin and thick, furry, shiny, and so on. Patterned bits can go together, and small items, such as braids and buttons, need a home of their own. For these, a set of transparent plastic kitchen storage units intended for holding sugar and rice is excellent.

Ordinary large glass storage jars can be used, too. It is important to store things so that you can easily see them.

How to start

For your first picture choose a simple design in a few colours on a plain background, such as the circles and squares design in this chapter. It's best not to try to be too realistic, or to aim for three dimensional effects to begin with, but to concentrate on colour and pattern.

Also, it's best at first not to have too many pieces overlapping each other, or you will become confused.

Choose the background material, and cut it a bit larger than the intended measurements of the finished picture; you can trim down more easily than you can add. The frame will cover a bit of the background all round the edge, so allow for this when you plan your design. For your first

attempt don't make the picture too big —about 12in by 15in or even smaller is a good size to start with. Iron all the fabrics flat before cutting out (except velvet, which should be steamed). Draw your design on paper. Then, either trace the design onto tracing paper, cut up the shapes and use them as a pattern for cutting out each shape, or cut up the drawing and use that as a pattern for the fabric. When you have more experience, you will be able to draw the shapes lightly in

pencil directly onto the fabric, or even cut out directly from the fabric. Place the background material onto a piece of card, and baste all round the edge one inch in to mark the overlap which will be needed for the mounting later.

Place all the fabric pieces in position on the background, and move them about a little to make sure that you are satisfied with the colour harmony and design.

Then pin them down.

Mark the position of each piece with a

pencil where it won't show as a guide to sticking them down.

Figures and complicated pieces of design are best done separately, then stuck down as a whole unit.

Using latex adhesives

Spread the adhesive on the smaller bits of fabric with a cocktail stick, and use a spreader for the larger pieces. The most important points to remember when using latex adhesives are not to use too much

and always to follow the directions on the container. Generally, the adhesive is spread thinly on one of the surfaces to be joined, then pressure is applied and the work allowed to dry. When fixing light-weight materials, apply latex sparingly to both surfaces and allow them to dry for a minute or two. Then place the two surfaces together. Nets can be stuck down success-fully by spreading the background itself with adhesive then pressing the net down onto it under a weight. If you do make a

mistake while sticking on fabrics most manufacturers of latex adhesives can supply a solvent which will remove it. Most clear adhesives can be removed with acetone, and most white adhesives can be removed with a damp cloth while they are tacky, or a petroleum solvent when dry.

Finishing off for framing

Press the finished work under a damp cloth—except areas where sequins may have been used. Cut the mounting card

an inch or so smaller than the background fabric, first making sure with a set square that all angles are right angles. Then, following the basted stitches as a guide, turn the edges of the background fabric back over the card, mitring the corners neatly, and lace the picture together at the back with strong thread. Easily frayed material can be pressed on to self-adhesive non-woven fabric before it is stuck down, or the edges can be overstitched, or a little glue can be run along the edges.

Felt jewellery

Pin a bunch of brilliant felt fruit on a beret, a lapel, a belt or use the motifs as appliqué shapes. Whatever you do, choose the brightest colours in felt and match them to the sharpest, sweetest shades in clothes and make-up . . . and above all wear them just for fun.

Felt is made in a mouth-watering range of zingy colours. It's easy to cut and sew and it's the ideal fabric to use for fun pin-on jewellery of all kinds. Try fruit brooches—a bright scarlet apple with vivid green leaves, a bunch of cherries, a big green pear—pinned on to a beret or a tee shirt.

Felt fruit is very simple to make. Trace the shapes from the graph (all shapes are the actual size) and stitch the two halves together with stab stitch or tiny running stitches. Most of the fruit and vegetable shapes shown here can be made from a piece of felt 4 inches square. The choker is made from a 14 inch by 1½ inch strip of cypress green felt, fastened with a small round button and a worked loop. Pipe cleaners, dyed with waterproof green ink, can be made into stalks and the stuffing for the fruit is cottonwool or kapok. Try embroidering leaf-veins and shadows in clever colours, use light beads or sequins for patches of highlight or pure decoration. Stitch small gilt safety pins to the backs of the brooches for fastenings.

54

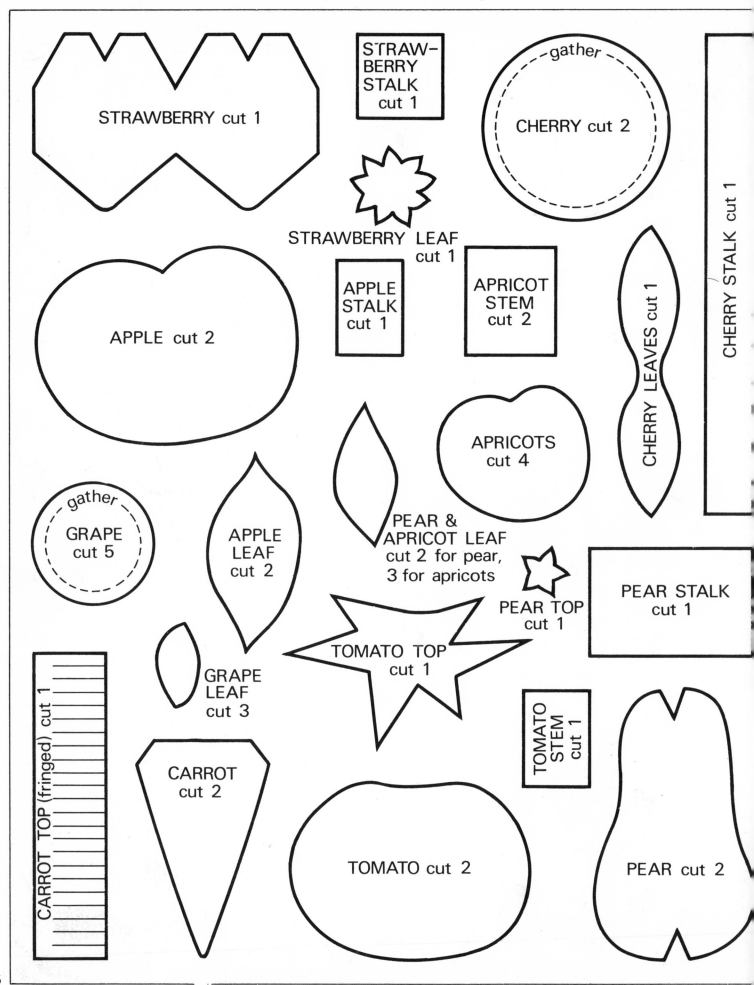

STRAWBERRY cut 1

STRAW-
BERRY
STALK
cut 1

gather
CHERRY cut 2

STRAWBERRY LEAF
cut 1

APPLE
STALK
cut 1

APRICOT
STEM
cut 2

CHERRY LEAVES cut 1

CHERRY STALK cut 1

APPLE cut 2

APRICOTS
cut 4

gather
GRAPE
cut 5

APPLE
LEAF
cut 2

PEAR &
APRICOT LEAF
cut 2 for pear,
3 for apricots

PEAR TOP
cut 1

PEAR STALK
cut 1

TOMATO TOP
cut 1

GRAPE
LEAF
cut 3

CARROT TOP (fringed) cut 1

TOMATO
STEM
cut 1

CARROT
cut 2

TOMATO cut 2

PEAR cut 2

CARROT

CHERRIES

STRAWBERRY

TOMATO

APPLE

PEAR

APRICOTS

GRAPES

Lace collage

Using odd scraps of lace and similar fabrics from your workbox you can, with a little care, build up beautiful collage pictures of flowers and trees.

Take a piece of lace

An odd table mat found at a jumble sale, a left-over length of lingerie trimming, a piece of lace bought in an antique shop, a scrap of crochet or knitting – these are often among the treasures hoarded away in sewing cupboards waiting for a chance to see the light of day.

The enchanting collages on these pages show a new way of using such lace scraps, or others which can be purchased quite cheaply from the needlework counters of large department stores.

▲ *A delicate flower piece that uses a knitted scrap for the vase, with flowers in muted tones of cream and white. Cream colours can be achieved by dipping lace in weak coffee or tea. Right: a charming tree landscape in which the shapes and colours have been carefully balanced* ▶

You will need

- ☐ An assortment of lace pieces
- ☐ Fabric adhesive
- ☐ Orange stick for applying adhesive
- ☐ Small paint brushes ☐ Scissors
- ☐ Colours. Water colours (used with plenty of water), coloured inks (for strong colours), coldwater dyes, (mixed and used like paints), or fabric paints are all suitable
- ☐ Mounting board. This can be white or coloured, depending on choice (fabric could be mounted on the board, for a textured background, as could blotting paper, which comes in a variety of attractive colours)

To make a lace picture

Cut out the pieces of lace, allowing them to suggest the subject of your picture, and compose the picture on a piece of rough paper. Move the pieces about until you arrive at a suitable design.

Try to keep the picture roughly to scale: a few large motifs amongst a lot of small ones could easily overwhelm them, and might be best on their own in a separate picture.

As the photographs show, compositions do not have to be large, nor does the subject matter have to be complicated.

The lace will lend itself to stylised rather than to realistic design.

When the subject and composition have been settled, the separate pieces of lace can be coloured (bearing in mind that the design may have to be changed slightly after colouring, because colour can drastically affect composition).

Choice of colour is very much a matter of personal preference. The ones shown here use subtle, harmonious colours to great effect, but there is no reason why brilliant colours should not be equally effective in their own way. Each lace section can have variations of colour within it, which will make for a more

vibrant picture than simply painting each piece in an even, flat colour. Lace can be left in its natural colour, then mounted on a coloured background, or colour can be used to emphasise different areas of two similar pieces of lace, thus adding variety to your raw materials. The possibilities are endless.

Mix the colour and paint it onto the lace. First try it out on a few spare pieces to make sure the colour is the right strength. Don't use thick, opaque paint or it will clog the surface of the lace and hide its texture.

Although it is necessary to colour only one side of the lace, the colour will soak through to the other side, so it is important to paint the lace on a temporary mounting, then transfer it to its final mounting when it is dry. Take a few measurements of the design while it is drying on its temporary mounting, and mark lightly with pencil where it is to go on its final mounting. This will make it easier to transfer.

Sticking

Use fabric adhesive sparingly, and apply to the larger areas with an orange stick. For the finer, lacier parts, lightly coat the back with adhesive, spreading it with the fingers to prevent it seeping through the spaces. Press into position when nearly dry.

Mounting

After the lace has been stuck down on its final mounting, the whole picture can be mounted on another piece of card, in a shade which picks out the dominant colour in the picture.

Frame behind glass.

◀ *Far left: a simple yet effective design using only three picees of lace. Above: Closely related shades of red, orange and yellow help to blend these lace flowers in a coherent design. The 'vase' is knitted* ▲

Lampshades

Choosing shapes

Lighting plays an important part in home decoration, and a well-placed lamp with a tastefully designed shade can contribute a great deal to the restful atmosphere and charm of almost any room. When considering a shade, choose a style, size and colour that will not be out of harmony with the lamp base.

Colours and lamp bases

Some colours are generally thought to be more suitable for lampshades than others. Good colours include gold, pink, red and green, although any colour is acceptable

The fashion revival for Tiffany lampshades is at the height of its popularity

if it fits into the colour scheme of the room and enhances the overall effect of the furnishings. Generally, blue and dead white shades tend to give a rather harder light than gold and red.

Bases for lamps require a lot of thought and it is advisable to take the base to the shop when choosing the shade frame, to see that the size and shape balance the base. A wide variety of ready-made bases are available but it is often possible to pick up a lovely old vase in your local junk shop and convert it. Old brass and silver candlesticks also make elegant bases and it is often worth spending a few dollars to have them properly converted. Wine

decanters and bottles rarely make good bases for lampshades.

Cover material and lining

When selecting cover material for a soft lampshade, choose a fabric with plenty of 'give', eg crepe back satin, rayon dupioni, wild silk and Thai silk. Heavy furnishing fabrics, cottons, nylons, and materials that do not stretch are not suitable for fitted lampshades.

Crepe back satin is the best choice for the lining as it has plenty of give, is reasonably priced, has a shiny surface to reflect the light, and is very easy to work. Jap silk is suitable for small shades only and it is

▲ *Instructions are given for making this empire lampshade*

Above left and right: first two stages in taping, figure 1

Above left and right: winding and finishing off

not as easy to use as crepe back satin.

The lining of a lampshade has two purposes; to hide the struts, particularly with pendant shades, and to give warmth to an otherwise cold light. A peach or pink lining, for instance, would give a warm glow to a white cover. Different effects can be achieved by using coloured linings. A white lining reflects the light and is a good choice when the cover material is dark.

Trimmings

Trimmings can make or mar a lampshade. Before deciding which trimming to use, first consider the type of lampshade being made and the room in which it is to be used. Tailored shades often look most effective with a plain trimming and are easily spoilt by a fussy one.

There are many attractive commercially-made trimmings from which to choose, in various widths and textures, but for a tailored effect try making the trimming

from a piece of crossway strip cut from the cover material. A well made and well applied crossway strip can look most elegant. It should be made with care and needs 'practice to make perfect', but is well worth the extra effort involved. Metallic braids and laces look well used in conjunction with a crossway strip trim.

Frames and fitting

The frame and fitting is the first consideration and is the basis of a successfully made lampshade.

Choose a frame made from a good firm wire (copper if possible) and one free from rough edges. If necessary file down any rough edges or they may poke through the binding tape. Check also that the frame is not bent because this is difficult to remedy.

It is advisable to paint the frame with a good gloss paint (allowing a day or two to dry thoroughly) as this reduces the risk of the frame rusting when it is washed.

Making an empire lampshade

To make a 10 inch bowed empire lampshade with a balloon lining you will need the following:

- ☐ Sharp pair of scissors
- ☐ Needles—sharps 9 for making silk shades
- ☐ Steel dressmaking pins or glass headed pins
- ☐ Good adhesive—UHU
- ☐ $\frac{3}{8}$in lampshade tape
- ☐ Soft pencil
- ☐ Thimble
- ☐ Matching silk
- ☐ $\frac{1}{2}$yd 36 inch fabric for the cover
- ☐ $\frac{1}{2}$yd 36 inch fabric for the lining

Binding the frame

This is a vital process in the making of a lampshade; if it is not done well, the cover and lining will be loose and baggy instead of taut and firm. For each strut allow twice its length in tape. For top

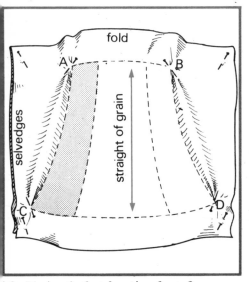

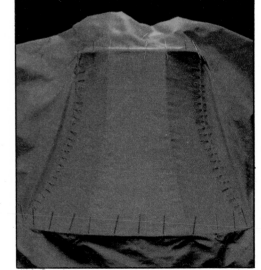

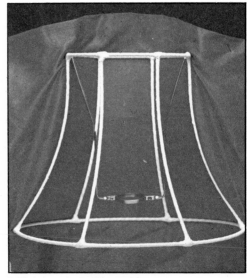

▲ **2.** *Placing the first four pins, figure 2*

▲ *Side struts, top and bottom pinned*

▲ *Showing the inside at this stage*

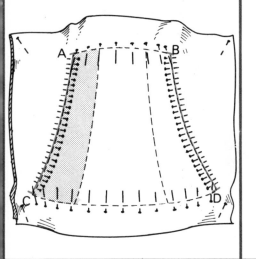

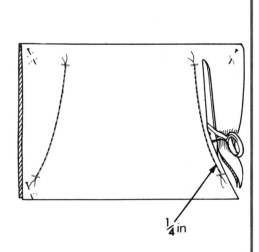

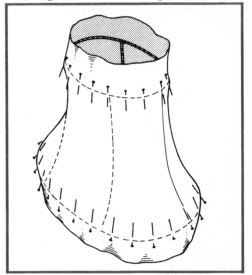

▲ **3.** *Marking struts with a pencil line*

▲ **4.** *Cutting along machining line*

▲ **5.** *Pinning top and bottom rings*

and bottom rings allow twice their circumference. If too much tape is used the struts become bulky and uneven.

Great care must be taken when taping the frame to ensure that the binding is both tight and smooth on the struts and rings. Tape each strut separately and then tape top and bottom rings. Always start and finish taping at the join of a strut and ring, otherwise the tape may work loose. Knot the tape exactly as illustrated. No sewing is necessary, except when braiding rings for hard lampshades where there are no struts (figure 1).

Fitting fabric onto frame

Fold the cover fabric in half and, with right sides together, place one pin in each corner to hold the pieces together. Place material onto one side only of the frame with the fold at the top and the grain running from the top of the frame to the bottom.

Place a pin at A, B, C, and D to hold

the fabric to the frame (figure 2).

Start pinning fabric to the side struts (AC and BD), placing pins in every $\frac{1}{2}$ inch. Do not pin on top and bottom rings yet, although some wrinkles will appear on the material. Check with the photograph illustrating this stage.

Make sure pins are placed on the side struts with the heads facing the center of the lampshade—this lessens the risk of damaging clothes and body. Now pin the top and bottom. Tighten the fabric as you go, just enough to remove the wrinkles, pinning every $1\frac{1}{2}$ inches and facing pins inwards. Complete pinning down the side struts by inserting pins every $\frac{1}{4}$ inch.

Mark down the struts over the pins with a soft pencil extending pencil line $\frac{1}{2}$ inch beyond the last pin on AB and CD and making a pencil mark $\frac{1}{2}$ inch round the top and bottom ring (figure 3).

Take out the pins from the frame but keep the holding corner pins in position.

Machine down the pencil line from top to bottom, using a medium-sized stitch; stretch fabric very slightly while doing this so that when it is pulled onto the frame the stitches do not break (figure 4).

Trim the fabric away $\frac{1}{4}$ inch from the stitching line at each side. Cut along the fold at the top edge but do not cut anything at the bottom.

Prepare the lampshade lining in exactly the same way.

Putting the cover on

Press the cover flat (do not press seams open) and slip it over frame with right side outside, making sure that the seams are placed on the side struts. Match horizontal pencil line to top and bottom rings. Pin top and bottom of side seams and then tighten fabric and pin every 1 inch round top and bottom rings (figure 5). Once again make sure that the pins are correctly placed to avoid unnecessary damage to clothes.

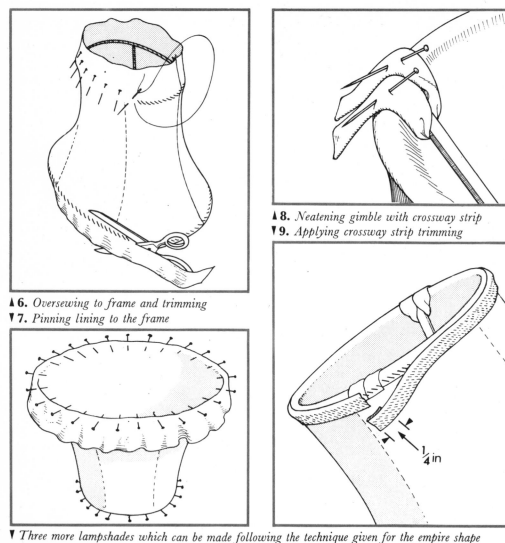

▲ **6.** *Oversewing to frame and trimming*
▼ **7.** *Pinning lining to the frame*

▲ **8.** *Neatening gimble with crossway strip*
▼ **9.** *Applying crossway strip trimming*

¼ in

▼ *Three more lampshades which can be made following the technique given for the empire shape*

Oversew the cover to the frame using a No.9 sharps needle and a short length of double matching silk thread. If too long a piece of thread is used it will catch round the pins; it is better to use several short lengths. The stitching should be on the outside edge of the top and bottom rings and the oversewing should be done from right to left. Trim away surplus material from top and bottom of lampshade, cutting right up to the stitches (figure 6).

Inserting balloon lining
Drop the prepared lining into the shade, matching seams and match horizontal pencil marks to top and bottom rings. Pin round top and bottom rings keeping pins on outside edge of lampshade (figure 7). Tighten the lining by adjusting the pins at top and bottom rings until there is no fullness left. Stitch lining in the same way as the cover, making sure that the stitches come on the outside edge of the lampshade. These will then be completely covered by the trimming.
Note: when fitting the fabric round the top ring, unpick the seam down to the horizontal pencil mark and splay out the material to enable the lining to fit neatly round the gimble. Do not try to join up material.

Neatening gimble
Cut a piece of crossway strip 1 inch wide and 4 inches long. Turn in ¼ inch at each side to make ½ inch wide strip. Press. Slip under gimble (figure 8). Pin in position and oversew in the same way as for the balloon lining, being careful to keep the stitches on the outside edge of the top ring.

Crossway trimming
Measure round top and bottom of lampshade and prepare enough crossway to fit round top and bottom of shade plus 2 inches for turnings. Prepare this in the same way as for neatening the gimble (figure 8). Make sure the material is cut on the direct cross and that any joins necessary are made on the cross.
Starting at the side seam apply end of crossway strip to outside edge of lampshade, beginning ¼ inch beyond seam.
Apply adhesive carefully and evenly to crossway strip, spreading with a small knife. Great care is needed in applying the adhesive, because it will mark the fabric if it is used carelessly.
Stretch the crossway strip slightly when applying it to the lampshade, pressing it gently with fingers to make it firm. The crossway should just cover the oversewing stitches and should not extend to the inside of the shade. When the strip has been

Two modern lampshades complement William Morris wallpapers, from the original pearwood blocks

applied to the top of the lampshade cut off the excess, turn under ¼ inch at one end and glue it over the other end (figure 9). Apply the trim to the bottom edge of the lampshade in the same way, making sure both joins are on the same side of the shade.

Hard lampshades

Hard lampshades are quick and easy to make, and attractive shades can be achieved with a minimum of effort. There are many attractive ready-made materials available from good handicraft shops, but it is also possible to make your own. Use an adhesive parchment to which the material of your choice can be ironed, pressing the material onto the adhesive side with a hot iron. If this method is used, it is advisable to use materials that will withstand a hot iron. The most suitable needles for making hard shades are between 5/6. A number of wooden clothes pegs are also required. The two lampshades illustrated on this page are hard lampshades. The one on the left requires a pattern; the other is the simplest of all shapes to make.

To make a drum lampshade

Two rings are used for a straight-sided drum lampshade. They must be the same size, but one should be plain and the other should have a fitting, pendant or gimble. Prepare the rings and tape as for the soft lampshade, finishing off the tape on the rings with a few oversewing stitches to keep it firm. Measure round the taped rings for the circumference and decide on the height required for the lampshade.

Cut a pattern from stiff paper or card to test on the rings. Allow ¼ inch at the end for the overlap at the seam.

Fit the paper pattern onto the rings with wooden clothes pegs and test the height of the shade and the fit of the pattern. Adjust if necessary. Cut fabric from the paper pattern and peg it onto the rings. Sewing from left to right and using a blanket stitch sew round top and bottom rings. Sew through the lampshade material and on to the tape. This gives a firm finish and the stitches will be covered by the trimming.

When top and bottom rings have been sewn the seam should be glued down. Press down firmly with fingers and hold until stuck.

With a good adhesive apply trimmings to top and bottom of shade, turning in ends ¼ inch and butting together. The joins of the trimming should be on the seam of the lampshade.

Making a pattern

This is the quickest and easiest way to obtain a pattern for a lampshade which is smaller at the top than at the bottom: ie a cone shape or near drum with side struts. Take a large sheet of card or stiff paper. Placing lampshade frame on paper, draw with a pencil down the side strut and mark top and bottom.

Rotate frame very slowly, marking along the top and bottom rings until the first mark is reached. Allow ½ inch for seam allowance at the end; this can be trimmed down to ¼ inch later. Cut out and try pattern onto frame, adjusting if necessary. Note: always try on the pattern before cutting into the lampshade fabric.

Cut out fabric from pattern and proceed in the same way as for the straight-sided drum.

This method can be used for making small wall light lampshades.

Tiffany lampshades

Unlined lampshade

Tailored cover

To calculate the amount of fabric, measure the circumference of the shade at its widest part and, if this is less than the width of the fabric, buy a piece equal to half the circumference. Otherwise buy a piece of the same measurement.

Cut the fabric across in two equal lengths and trim them to make two squares. With the 'right' sides together, place both pieces over one half of the frame with one corner of the fabric at the top. Pin it to the rings at points A and B. (Fig.3). Smooth out the fabric towards the bound struts and pin the fabric to them at the top and bottom. Easing away as much fullness as possible, pin the fabric down the struts, placing the pins at right angles. Pin along the rings, evening out any fullness (Fig.4).

Follow the line of the bound struts, mark the fitting line with pins or basting, taking care not to catch the binding. Mark the lines of the rings in the same way. Unpin the fabric from the frame and, following the fitting lines of the struts,

machine stitch the pieces together along these lines only (Fig.5). Trim off the excess fabric to within ¼in. of the stitching and press the seam over to one side. Neaten the raw edges by overcasting them together. Remove the binding from the struts.

Place the cover, 'right' side out, over the frame and position it so that the seams are over the struts. Tuck the seams behind them. Pin the fabric to the ring at the top of the seams, smooth tightly down to the bottom and pin again (do not pin it down the length of the strut or you may leave pinholes).

Next, stretching and adjusting the fabric as you go, pin the fabric all round the rings, easing

in any fullness. Then oversew it to both rings, beginning at the base (Fig.6). Turn the surplus fabric back over the stitching, clipping where necessary, and stitch again (Fig.7). Cut off the excess fabric as close as possible to this second row of stitches.

Semi-fitted cover

Cut out a strip of fabric, on the straight grain, with the width equal to the height of the frame plus 2in., and with the length equal to the circumference of the frame plus ½in. Make a tube by joining the short ends of the strip together with a plain seam. Trim the seam allowance to within ¼in. of the stitching, press the seam over to one side and neaten the raw edges by overcasting them together. Fit the tube over the

frame, positioning the seam over a strut. Pin it to both rings, gathering the fabric to fit it to the top ring. Stitch it firmly, as above.

Lined Tiffany

Lining a Tiffany lampshade is fairly 'fiddly', but well worth doing if the shade is to hang from the ceiling. Although the lining can be cut out and made up as for the tailored cover (see above), it is slightly easier if you cut it in four sections by fitting the fabric—on the bias grain—to the 1st and 4th bound struts. Mark the seam line as above and also mark the lines of the unbound struts. Cut out and mark the other sections in the same way and join them together.

With the 'wrong' side facing outwards, place the lining inside the frame, positioning it so

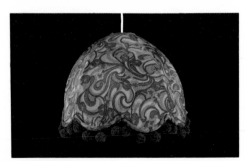

that the seams correspond with the bound struts. Pin the lining to the rings and along the bound struts, adjusting and easing the fabric as you go. Oversew the lining to the bound struts, and along the rings.

To prevent the lining from looking 'baggy' on the inside, you will also have to catch the lining to the unbound struts. Place one hand inside the frame and hold the lining to one strut. Starting at the top, secure the sewing thread to the binding on the ring. Working from the outside, take a tiny stitch in the lining on the basted guide line about ¼in. from the top. Bring the needle out on the other side of the strut and pass it back over the strut and under the loop

made by the thread (rather like blanket stitch, see Fig.8).

Continue down the strut, loosely catching the lining to the strut in this way at ½in. intervals. Leave the end of thread free at the bottom of the strut and start again on the next strut.

When all the unbound struts have been attached to the lining in this way, it is possible to adjust the positioning by sliding the stitches along the strut. Tighten the stitches from the loose end and then secure the thread.

When you attach the cover, place its edge over the edge and stitching of the lining.

If the cover is a semi-fitted one, it is possible to attach it to the frame so that no stitching shows on the outside, making a trimming un-

necessary. With the wrong side of the cover facing out, and the bottom of the cover uppermost, fit this edge over the bottom ring of the frame. Taking a ¼in. turning, oversew the cover to the bottom ring (Fig.9). Then turn the cover up and over the frame and fit and stitch it to the top ring as above.

Trimming

Pin the trimming to the cover at top and bottom, covering the raw edges. Stitch it to the cover on both edges, working from side to side, and taking the thread underneath the trimming. Stitch a second piece of trimming inside the frame if you wish to cover the binding.

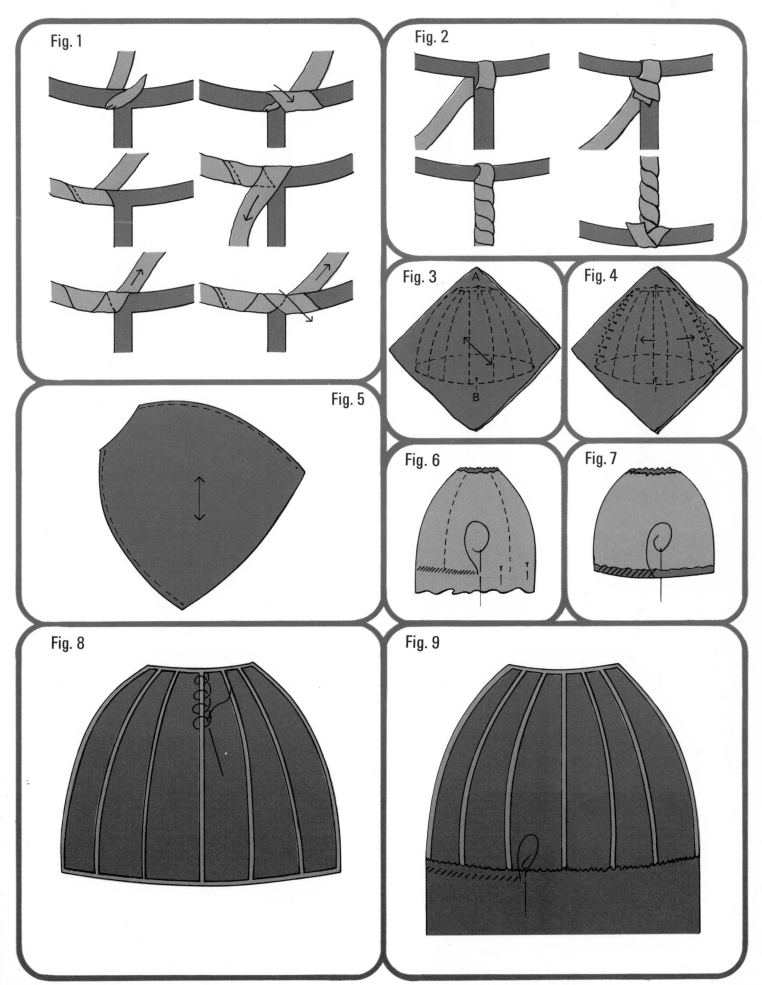

Fig. 1

Fig. 2

Fig. 3

Fig. 4

Fig. 5

Fig. 6

Fig. 7

Fig. 8

Fig. 9

Natural dyes

Although natural dyeing takes longer than synthetic dyeing, the colours obtained are often more attractive than those produced by modern chemical dyes. Natural dyes produce a certain lustre and softness in the fabric or yarn they are applied to that chemicals do not give, and it is rewarding, too, to select plants or berries from the garden or hedgerow and use them to produce a beautifully coloured yarn or fabric.

Most plants will produce staining juices if crushed and boiled, but comparatively few produce a fast dye when applied to fabric or yarn. Some of these plants produce staining juices which are known as 'adjective' or 'mordant' dyes: that is the fabric or yarn to be dyed must be subjected to a preparatory bath containing a metallic mineral, or mordant, to enable the dye to penetrate the yarn fibres. There are also a few substantive, or non-mordant dyes that do not require a fixing agent. These include the lichens and walnuts. In most cases, however, mordanting is a vital process, for an unevenly mordanted yarn or fabric will not dye evenly.

Wool is easy to mordant, as the fibres are porous, but silk, cotton and linen are more difficult; silk has to be steeped for a long time in a tepid or cold mordant, and often loses its lustre, and cotton and linen fibres are so tough that it is difficult to get the mordant to penetrate evenly. For the beginner, then, wool is the best fibre to dye.

Wool to be dyed must be put through the following processes: scouring (washing, to remove any dust or grease), mordanting and dyeing.

Different mordants can produce a darker or brighter dye effect, besides preparing the fabric for the dye.

Mordants

There are many mordants, but the three most commonly used are the following:

Potassium aluminium sulphate (alum)
This is the most commonly used mordant. Use 4 oz, dissolved in a little cold water with 1 oz cream of tartar, per lb of thick wool, and 3 oz with 1 oz cream of tartar, for thin wool. This produces clear colours.

Bichromate of potash (chrome)
This mordant gives wool a soft and silky feel, mellowing the shade. Use ½ oz chrome with 1 oz cream of tartar to 1 lb of wool. A lid should be placed on the mordant bath, as chrome is very sensitive to light. The wool should not be exposed to light after mordanting. It should be rinsed and, if it is not to be dyed immediately, shut in a drawer or put in a linen bag.

Stannous chloride (tin)
Tin can be used as a mordant, or it can be added to a dyebath towards the end of dyeing to brighten the colour. It should always be carefully dissolved before adding to a dyebath made of galvanised iron, as it destroys the surface of the vessel. Used as a mordant, the ratio is ½ oz tin and 2 oz cream of tartar to 1 lb of wool, used as for alum. The cream of tartar should be dissolved in water before adding the tin. To brighten a shade, a few tin crystals should be added to an alum mordant.

Dyeing equipment

You will need
- [ ] 1 lb of the natural dye of your choice per 1 lb dry weight of yarn or fabric
- [ ] 2 galvanised iron, enamel or stainless steel buckets (one for dye, one for mordanting)
- [ ] 1 packet soap flakes (*not* chemical detergent)
- [ ] Kitchen scales
- [ ] Water thermometer
- [ ] Smooth wood sticks to handle yarn or fabric during dyeing
- [ ] The mordant of your choice
- [ ] Cream of tartar

The mordanting process

Preparation
Wool must be thoroughly washed, or scoured, before being mordanted and

These colours were obtained from a range of common plants including walnut skins, privet leaves, gorse flowers, marsh marigold flowers, dog's mercury, blackberry shoots, onion skins, bracken, lichens and oak bark ▼

◄ *An Egyptian rug woven by hand in naturally dyed wools*

BLACKBERRY

PRIVET

RAGWORT

WALNUT

GORSE

HEATHER

ONION

GROUND ELDER

SLOE

ELDERBERRY

dyed, to remove all fat and dirt. If this is not done the colour cannot be fast as the dirt and grease absorb the dye. Steep the wool in hot water until thoroughly soaked, then allow to cool. Work up a warm soap lather in a bucket, immerse the wool and work it very gently. Rinse in water of the same temperature, then repeat the process, treating the wool gently at all times. Squeeze, but do not

twist. The wool can be mordanted while still damp.

Skeins of wool should be tied in a loose figure-of-eight tie, so the mordant can penetrate to all parts easily. Be careful that they are not too tightly tied, or the mordant will not soak in and the result will be white patches on the wool after dyeing.

Make sure the mordant is quite dissolved

before putting in the yarn, or there may be bad stains on the finished article. Always see that the saucepan or bucket is quite big enough for the yarn and do not stir too vigorously or the wool will become 'felted'.

The process

Dissolve the appropriate amount of mordant and cream of tartar in a little cold water and add to a large bucket of cool water. Stir well, and heat. Remember that chrome mordant must be covered, as it is sensitive to light. As the water warms, add the wool, which should be wetted beforehand, and bring slowly to boiling point. Then let it simmer: one hour for thick yarn or fabric, three-quarters of an hour for finer qualities. Lift out the wool with a smooth wood stick and let it drain for a moment. Squeeze excess moisture from it but do not wring or wash it. The wool can be dyed immediately, but is better left in a linen bag overnight, or longer.

Dyes

The usual quantity necessary to produce a medium shade of a natural dye is 1 lb of dye-plant to 1 lb dry weight of yarn or fabric.

To prepare a dye

Most dye-plants need to be crushed (berries) or chopped (leaves, flowers or stems), added to a bucket of cold water and then heated. When boiling point is reached, the dye is simmered for a time. Most dyes are then allowed to cool and left to stand overnight.

Dyeing wool

Having chosen and prepared the dye of your choice, follow the instructions given for that dye. After the wool is lifted from the bath, the excess dye should be gently squeezed from it, and the wool rinsed until the water runs clear. A hot soapy wash will then improve and set the colour, after which the yarn or fabric should be dried.

Plants used in dyeing

Birch bark

Birch bark should be chopped up small, added to cold water, heated, then when boiling point is reached, simmered for two to three hours. Leave to cool, let it stand overnight, then add the fabric or yarn to be dyed, bring back to the boil and simmer until the required depth of colour is reached. Birch bark produces plum colour, which becomes brown with the addition of iron mordant and a dull, deep gold with alum.

Blackberries

The young shoots of blackberries, picked in spring, should be boiled with the yarn for an hour or more, iron mordant and cream of tartar added (see mordant chart for amounts) and dyeing continued for half an hour to yield a deep, almost black colour. The berries, which produce a bluish-grey colour, should be

crushed, put in cold water and brought to the boil. The yarn, which should be mordanted with alum before immersion, is placed in the dye and simmered until the required depth of colour is obtained.

Bracken shoots

Pick the shoots in spring while they are still curled, put in cold water, bring gradually to the boil and simmer for two hours, then cool. Use alum mordant on the yarn to be dyed; place this, after mordanting, in the dye, and simmer again for two hours. This produces a clear, yellowish-green colour.

Dog's mercury

The whole plant can be used. Should be gathered in early spring and chopped before being added to cold water in the dyebath and brought to the boil. Use 2 lb of the plant to 1 lb of wool. Alum mordant should be used on the yarn to be dyed. Immerse the mordanted yarn when dye is boiling and simmer until the desired colour is reached. Produces a yellow-green colour.

Elder

The leaves give a green colour, treated as for birch bark and used on alum mordanted yarn. The berries give a lilac-blue colour with alum mordanted yarn with 1 oz salt added to the mordant, and a violet colour with alum mordant alone. Prepare as for privet berries.

Gorse flowers

Gorse flowers can be used alone or with young shoots. Boil the flowers or young shoots for one hour, strain, and add to a dyebath half-full of cold water. Use 1 lb of the plant to 1 lb of yarn. Repeat the process and add yarn that has been mordanted with alum, simmering until the desired colour is reached. Produces a strong yellow.

Heather shoots

Ling is the best type of heather to use. Bring it gradually to the boil, simmer for three to four hours, cool and stand overnight. Alum mordant should be used on the yarn to be dyed (4 oz alum and 2 oz cream of tartar to 1 lb of yarn), which should then be added to the dyebath. Bring this back to the boil, and simmer for one hour. Produces olive yellow.

Lichens (non-mordant)

Lichens should be scraped off walls or rocks, well bruised and crumbled, if dry. Put alternate layers of lichen and yarn into the dyebath. Fill the dyebath with cool water and bring slowly to the boil. Simmer for some hours until the

required depth of colour is reached. Wash well. The colour will be very fast and range from dark auburn brown to pinky orange or pale yellow.

Onion skins

Use only the outer skins. Boil for about two hours and then immerse the yarn, which should have been mordanted with alum. This produces golden brown. Tin added towards the end of dyeing produces orange brown. Hang the yarn in the open air to remove the smell. Not a very durable dye.

Privet berries

Crush the berries before adding them to a dyebath of cold water (1½ lb berries to 1 lb yarn) and use alum mordant on the yarn to be dyed. Dye as for birch bark. Produces a bluish green.

Privet leaves

Soak leaves overnight in cold water. Bring gradually to the boil and simmer for thirty minutes. Strain and cool. Proceed as for birch bark, with alum mordanted yarn. Produces a yellow colour.

Ragwort

Chop flower heads into small pieces. Put into a bucket of cold water; bring gradually to the boil and simmer for two to three hours. Allow to grow cold. Next day, heat again, to just below boiling point, immerse alum mordanted yarn and simmer until required depth of colour is reached.

Sloe berries

Treat as for privet berries. Produces slate blue.

Walnuts (non-mordant)

Collect when ripe, put in a cask and cover with water. Leave for several weeks and use the liquid as a dye, when required. No mordant is necessary. A brown colour is obtained; the longer the walnuts are left in the cask, the darker the colour. The husks can be boiled for half an hour and allowed to cool. The yarn is then immersed and the dye is boiled until the desired shade is reached.

Weld (wild mignonette)

The plants should be gathered before seeding. The whole plant except the root is dried and chopped up small, placed in a bucket of cold water, simmered for several hours and cooled, before dyeing proceeds. Weld on an alum mordanted yarn gives lemon yellow and on chrome gives golden yellow. With tin it gives yellow orange and, with iron, olive yellow.

73

SIR CHRISTOPHER
WREN
TOOK UP HIS PEN
AND WORKED
FOR HOURS
ON THE CITY TOWERS

YOU CAN
VISIT THEM STILL
WITHOUT ANY FUSS
BY
LONDON TRANSPORT
TRAIN OR BUS

Paper sculpture

This superb coloured paper sculpture of Christopher Wren was designed for a London Transport poster

Many people have tried their hand at papercraft at some time or another, either as children, or later when they've attempted to make a paper flower, or perhaps tried to fold a paper napkin attractively for a party table. This chapter is about the art of folding and bending paper to produce three-dimensional effects.

The limitations imposed by using paper as a raw material are in a way an advantage, especially to the beginner. It is impossible to reproduce realistically in paper, so one is compelled to use imagination and originality and interpret what is seen in stylised form.

Once a few simple rules and techniques have been mastered, there is no limit to the wonderful objects and designs that can be made—table decorations, lamp shades, masks, standing figures, animals, pictures in frames, fancy dresses, wall plaques, hanging mobiles—even stage scenery. Paper is surprisingly robust when treated correctly, and creations made from it will last as long they are needed.

Materials and tools

Paper. There are dozens of different types of paper on the market, and it's important to choose one that is right for the work in hand. For a large relief thin mounting card is used, and for a small, light piece of work a good quality thick cartridge

▲ *A sturdy London policeman, made in paper for a magazine promotion* ▲ *Penguin in paper sculpture designed for a paper company promotion*

paper is best. Anything thinner than this is unsuitable because the paper will not stand up under its own weight, nor will it bend or fold properly. Above all, paper must be of good quality, strong enough to stand well, and sufficiently pliable to bend easily.

Foil-covered and surfaced papers, coloured papers and those coloured on one side only can be most effective for paper craft, although scoring is likely to expose the white backing on the latter. If only white paper is obtainable, and a coloured effect is required, spray-paint the paper before starting or paint the sculpture when it is completed. Never mix white papers in one piece of work unless a contrast is required. There are several different shades of white and one will clearly show against another.

Scissors. These should be sharp. It is best to have two pairs, a large pair for cutting big areas, and a small, pointed pair for delicate, detailed work.

Knife. For a cleaner cut, many people

use a blade in preference to scissors, but it is a matter of personal choice. If a blade is used, it must be sharp, and because pressure will be exerted on it a guard of some kind is essential. A stencil knife is ideal. A scalpel blade is also recommended—obtainable with a special holder, or a proper cutting tool with changeable blades. These are all available at craft shops. Razor blades are not recommended because they break under pressure.

Scoring tool. Scoring is an important part of paper sculpture and tools are obtainable from Art and craft shops. A suitable scoring tool can be made by fixing a blunt darning needle into a pen holder, or even by tying one to a pencil

Adhesives. A clear cellulose acetate glue is best for sticking paper. Rubber solution can be used and is easily removed by rubbing off when dry.

Paper can also be stuck together with double-sided paper tape, which is less messy than glue, and can also be used to

reinforce delicate areas.

Ruler. A metal ruler or one with a metal edge on one side is necessary to cut against. Wooden or plastic rulers without a metal edge should not be used for cutting, because there is a danger with these that the knife will skid onto the ruler and cut the fingers.

Set Square. For true right angles.

Compasses. For drawing circles.

Pencils. An HB pencil is probably the best to use. Anything softer will smudge and wear down quickly, and anything harder will make a line that is too faint to see. Keep pencils well sharpened.

Cutting board. Either use a piece of hardboard or an old pastry board but do not use boards with a noticeable grain. Cover the cutting board with thick paper and cut out on this, replacing the paper when necessary.

Handling paper and glue

Cutting. When cutting paper into a shape first mark the line to be cut in

76

pencil. Then cut against the metal edge of the ruler, cutting evenly and gently three or four times along the marked line until unwanted paper falls away, rather than trying to exert heavy pressure on the knife, and doing it all in one go.

Scoring. Scoring is an important part of paper work, enabling thick pieces of card and paper to be folded without breaking or wrinkling. Scoring is simply cutting half-way through the paper. Mark the line to be cut in pencil, place the ruler against it as for cutting, then cut without exerting very much pressure. With scoring and folding, sharp, clear-cut effects of light and shade can be obtained.

Curling. Sometimes a design may call for a piece of paper to bend gracefully and this means curling the paper. If you are right-handed, hold the paper to be curled in the left hand, and a ruler or a scissor blade in the right hand. Place the implement under the edge of the piece of paper, securing it by placing the thumb of the right hand on top of it. Still holding the paper firmly on the ruler with your thumb, draw the ruler away and towards the edge of the paper. It will curl away from the thumb and down over the ruler or blade (see illustration). Curling gives soft, gentle effects of light and shade.

Applying adhesives

Keep paper, hands and tools scrupulously clean while working and try not to get adhesives on the fingers. Keep adhesives capped when not actually in use and use a spreader wherever possible. A narrow strip of card, cut into four inch lengths, makes effective spreaders for small areas, and a toothpick is also useful for applying dots of adhesive.

An important rule to remember—don't swamp the work with glue; it doesn't necessarily result in a better bond. Two sparingly gummed surfaces left to partially dry will fix quite firmly.

Simple projects

Try the following folds and cuts and observe the shapes and effects which result. Make some basic forms, boxes, hexagons and cones and vary the surfaces with fan pleats. Concave pleats are made by scoring the paper on the surface and convex pleats by scoring on the underside. For rounded shapes give the paper a cylindrical bias by drawing the paper under a ruler before starting to fold and score.

Try each fold and cut and see what effects are achieved. The diagram extreme right bottom illustrates the method for curling paper.

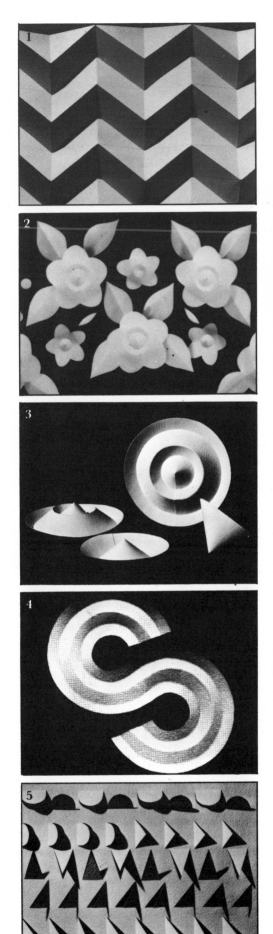

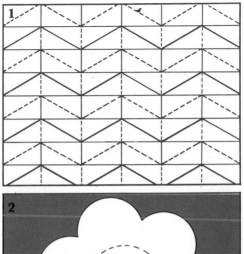

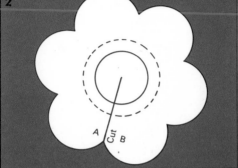

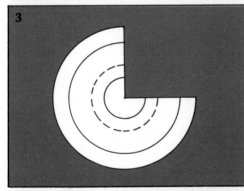

Curling paper

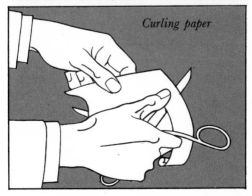

Shadow folds

Score diagonal lines on one side of the paper, reversing it to press in sharp creases. Scoring and creasing are indicated by a solid line for the right side of the paper and a dotted line for the back of the paper. Curvy or wavy folds are made by scoring a reversed curved line followed by a parallel curved line, scoring on alternate sides of the paper.

Different patterns can be made by varying the depth or shape of the folds (figure 1).

Cut surface designs

Cutting into paper at regular intervals gives a design of light and shadow, useful for indicating fish scales, feathers, leaves, etc.

Another useful effect can be created by raising the cuts and placing darker or coloured paper underneath the design. Patterns can be drawn geometrically, but for texture designs such as feather effects they are best cut freely (figure 5).

Cone formation

To make a cone, draw a circle and cut out. Remove a segment and join the edges together. The circle in the diagram has three inner circles, two drawn on one side

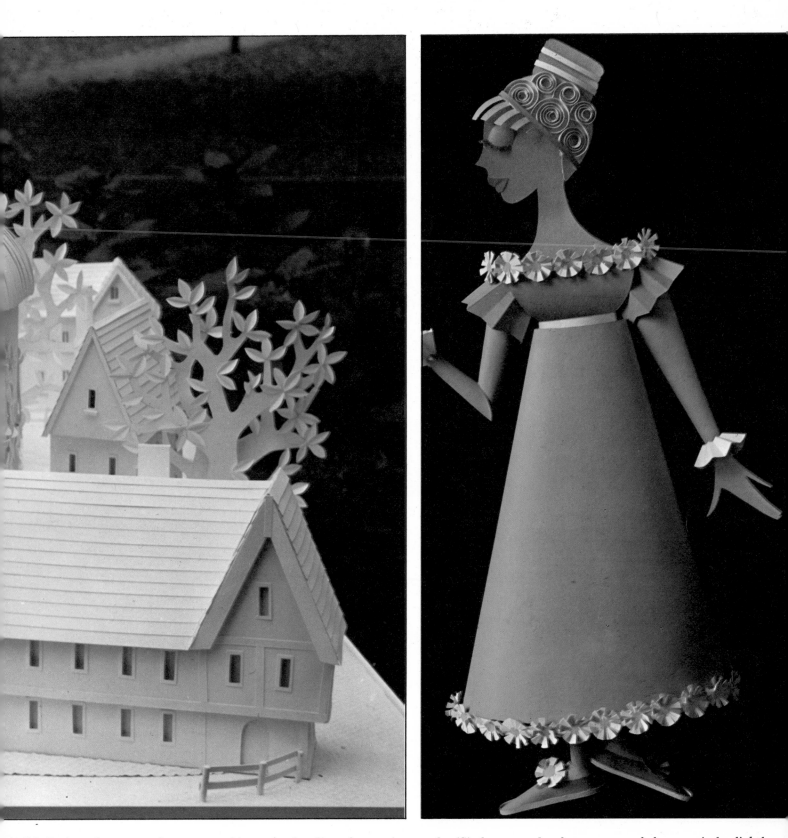

(solid line) and one on the reverse side (dotted line). Score these circles and cut out a quarter segment. Bend the scoring on both sides, mould into a cone and secure (figure 3).

Curves

For curves, first draw an 'S' formation and cut out. Score with a knife down the centre, following the shape and mould by bending the scoring to the 'S' shape. This multi-scoring and moulding strengthens the paper, and these curved pieces can be made into many beautiful and different forms (figure 4).

Stylised flower

Draw a flower shape from the diagram, cut out and draw a circle on one side of the paper (shown as a solid line). Turn the shape over and draw a circle slightly larger than the first (shown as a dotted line). Score both circles, one on each side of the paper, and cut between two petals from the outside edge to the center of flower. Pull 'A' over 'B', covering one whole petal and glue. Crease the center scoring to make a deep cone. Small flowers are made, with only one circle scored in the center (figure 2).

Pasta collage

Pasta, the Italian word for food made from flour, eggs and water, makes a delicious meal, but it can also be used to create delightful pictures. Spaghetti and macaroni are the most familiar types of pasta, but it comes in a wide selection of unusual and interesting shapes which can be used in the fascinating craft of pasta pictures. Seeds, lentils and beans can be used, too, to add variety. The pasta shapes are stuck to a hard backing in attractive designs, and then sprayed with gold, silver or ordinary aerosol gloss paint.

Designing with pasta

The shapes of the type of pasta chosen will obviously influence the design, but plan a bold pattern, avoiding a lot of intricate detail. The charm of a pasta picture lies in the grouping of different textures and the swirling forms that can be achieved with them, many of which will be suggested by the pasta itself. Therefore, aim for abstract or semi-abstract design.

You will need:
- [ ] A base of chipboard or some other firm material that does not bend or warp (not polystyrene, as the spray paint will dissolve it)
- [ ] Undercoat or glue size to prime the base
- [ ] Soft pencil
- [ ] Tape measure or ruler
- [ ] Adhesive, such as Evo-Stik or white glue
- [ ] Several varieties of raw pasta
- [ ] Tweezers, for handling pasta
- [ ] An orange stick to move pieces of pasta about on the base
- [ ] Aerosol gloss paint or varnish, *not* polyurethane

Raw pasta, available in many interesting shapes, some of which are shown here, can be used in the craft of pasta pictures. Seeds, lentils and beans can be added, for variety

Preparing the base

Paint the chipboard base with under-coat or glue size, to prime. This is important as the chipboard is absorbent and will dry a different colour from the pasta after the final spraying if it is not treated. Allow to dry, then mark a faint borderline in pencil, about 2 inches in from the edge of the base, all around, and keep the pasta design inside this. The border will make the picture easier to handle, and enable you to frame the pasta picture.

Draw your chosen design carefully onto the board, defining the main areas that are to be covered with pasta. If you have chosen a symmetrical design, ensure that the measurements are accurate by working the angles out with a tape measure or ruler. It is not necessary to fill in all parts of the design with pasta; blank spaces can add to the effect.

Fixing the pasta

Place the board on a flat working surface and arrange the pasta, which can be augmented by dried peas, lentils and dried beans, in groups to one side of the board. Then proceed in one of two ways: either arrange the pasta design, unglued, on the board, using tweezers to handle it, then remove small portions of the design at a time, glue them and replace them on the board, or glue a small area of the design and stick the pasta straight down, without arranging the whole design first. It is best

to try out the design first, to see if it looks right, before glueing it down. Try not to leave trails of adhesive over the pasta or the board, because it is likely to show when work is completed. Allow the adhesive to dry overnight, if possible, before painting. Test to make sure the pasta is firmly glued, before painting.

Painting the pasta

Pasta pictures can be left in their natural yellowish colour and look very effective on a contrasting background. Usually, however, pasta pictures are given a coat of aerosol gloss paint, or varnish to finish them. Polyurethane varnish should not be used, as it will cause the pasta to deteriorate. Spraying

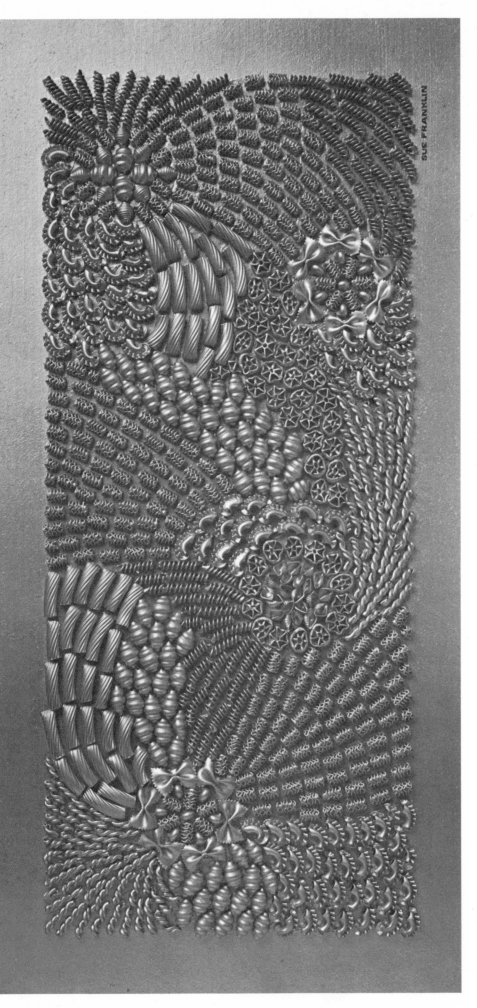

SUE FRANKLIN

◄ *The effective use of gold paint*
▼ *A detail of picture, left, reveals textures*

82

▲ *A brilliant red panel in a striking design like an 'exploding sun'*

▼ *Dramatic bronze-coloured panels*

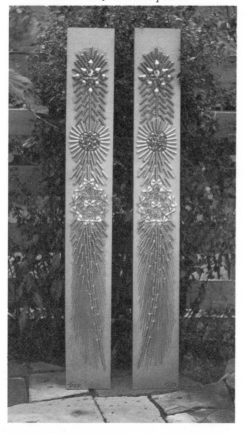

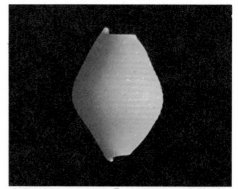

▲ *Shells—conquilli* ▼ *Twists—tortiglioni*

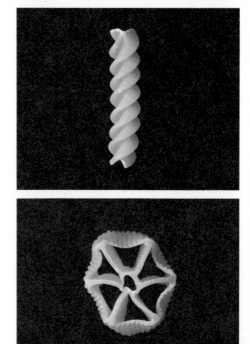

▲ *Wheels—ruote de carro* ▼ *Butterflies—farfalle*

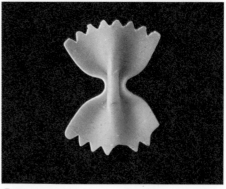

▼ *Crest of a hen—cresto di gallo*

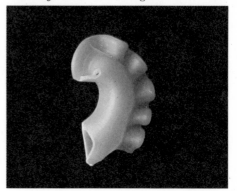

paint on top of a coat of varnish is not advisable.

The finish that is most successful is that of spray gloss paint in a colour, or one of the many excellent metallic finishes available, such as bronze, silver, gold or copper.

Obviously, it takes a very long time to paint a pasta picture by hand, as the pasta is so intricate in shape, but it is possible to mask off certain parts of the picture, spraying the unmasked area with a single colour and afterwards masking out other areas and respraying. Two or three different coats of paint can be sprayed over each other for depth of colour or variation in tone.

For an interesting rough texture drop silver or coloured sand onto the newly varnished or painted surface of the pasta.

Pasta is inclined to break easily, both while it is being stuck into a design and after completion, so, unless a pasta picture is protected by glass, it cannot be regarded as permanent. It is easier, therefore, to frame and glaze pasta pictures, which also helps to protect the surface from dust.

Patchwork

Patchwork was originally regarded as an economical way of using up scraps. Later it became an art form, and with imaginative use of colour and clever use of shapes, textures and patterns, it makes original and beautiful pieces of needlework.

Basic shapes in patchwork

The basic shapes used in patchwork are mostly geometric; squares, diamonds, triangles, hexagons, oblongs, and octagons. The straight sides of these shapes make them easy to stitch together and, if strongly contrasting colours and tones are used, interesting three-dimensional effects can be built up in patchwork designs. The clamshell is very effective but more difficult to make up and cannot be used with the geometric shapes.

Fabrics for patchwork

Cotton is the most satisfactory fabric because it is available in a wide variety of colours and patterns, launders easily and isn't inclined to fray. Synthetic fabrics can be used for patchwork but care has to be taken because many novelty fabrics fray and stretch. For a rich, luxurious look, pure silk makes superb patchwork but don't use it for articles which are likely to get a lot of wear. Velvet makes opulent patchwork, particularly when it is used with metallic braids, but it isn't easy to work

with. The pile is inclined to make the fabric 'creep', which makes difficulties when putting on the paper backing and preparing for stitching. If you do use velvet, remember that the direction of the pile has to be taken into account.

Wool fabrics and tweeds make unusually beautiful patchwork for home furnishings and fashion accessories. The textures and colours can produce a delightful homespun look but loosely woven fabrics must be avoided.

It is important to remember that, when different types of fabrics are being used in a piece of patchwork, the weights of the various kinds must be similar or the patchwork will pucker or pieces may pull apart after they have been stitched.

Preparing fabric for patchwork

For articles which are likely to require frequent laundering, pre-shrunk fabric should be chosen. If you are using up old scraps of washable fabric, it's a wise precaution to wash all the pieces before starting, to shrink them and to check for fast colours.

Uses for patchwork

Patchwork can be used to make home furnishings, accessories, toys and all kinds of small gifts. Bands of patchwork can be used as appliqué for curtains, cushions and bedspreads and for trimming clothes. If a large area is made up

and then used as a piece of fabric for dressmaking, colourful and exciting clothes can be made, such as the Happi coat illustrated.

Preparing for patchwork

The fabric shapes for patchwork are cut out with the help of a template and then are backed with paper to keep them firm while they are being stitched. Templates can be purchased but you can make your own from the shapes given here, cutting them out of stiff card. Ideally, templates should be made of metal, Perspex or wood and perhaps a handyman will make a set for you from the shapes given.

Make two templates of the shape chosen; one exactly to the size given and the other $\frac{1}{4}$ inch larger all round.

The first template is for cutting out paper shapes, the second is for cutting out the fabric pieces, which have to have a seam allowance all round. If the second template is not made of a transparent substance, it is quite useful to cut a window in it so that you can move it about on patterned fabrics to choose the best part of the fabric design, or to center a motif on a patch. The backing used for the patches should be of fairly stiff paper, so that the patches are kept firm in working. Strong brown paper, greetings cards or magazine covers are ideal. The paper shapes must be accurately cut or the finished patchwork will not lie flat.

To prepare patches for joining

Cut paper and fabric shapes. Pin a paper shape to the wrong side of a fabric patch, placing the paper so that

These beautiful silk patchwork cushions give a splendidly rich look to an otherwise simple setting

◄ *This detail from an eighteenth-century English bedspread shows the superb result of combining patchwork and embroidery techniques*

the turnings are exactly equal on all sides. Fold the turnings on to the paper, pulling the fabric gently taut, and baste the fabric to the patch. Don't use a knot or a backstitch, simply catch the thread end under one of the stitches. Remove the pins after basting. Prepare a number of patches in the same way, ready for joining.

Joining patches

There are three methods of joining patches; by straight machine stitching, (figures 1, 2 and 3), by machine zigzag stitch and by hand. To join patches by hand, place two backed patches together, right sides facing, with edges carefully matched. Oversew along one edge, using a fine needle and matching thread. Never pull an edge to fit if it doesn't match up. Unpick the patch and start again.

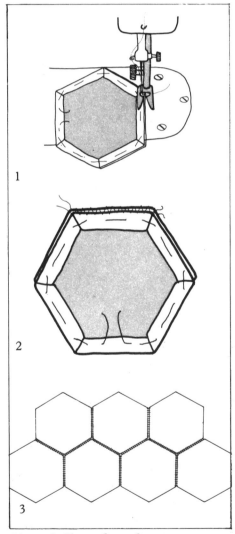

Clamshell patchwork

Clamshell patches are overlapped, like the scales of a fish (figure 4). Clamshell 'work differs from traditional patchwork in that the stitching is done from the right side, as in appliqué work. As the patches have a curved edge, a supple and fairly fine fabric must be used; too

The Happi coat, in bold bright cotton squares, is fun to make and wear

thick a fabric will not take the smooth curve, It is most important that the papers are pinned to the fabric with the grain of the fabric running down the length of the patch. This helps the patches to lie flat when they are joined. Each clamshell patch should have a $\frac{3}{8}$ inch to $\frac{1}{2}$ inch turnings allowance.

The turnings are pleated and not gathered, and the pleats must be regular, so that there are no bumps or uneven parts on the curve (figure 5).

Clamshell patches are joined in overlapping rows, right sides out, with the curved top of the first row of patches worked along against a straight edge (figure 4). The second row of patches is laid over the lower part of the first row of clamshells and basted in position. The first two rows are then sewn

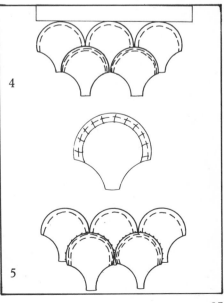

This unfinished example of nineteenth-century patchwork still retains the original basting threads

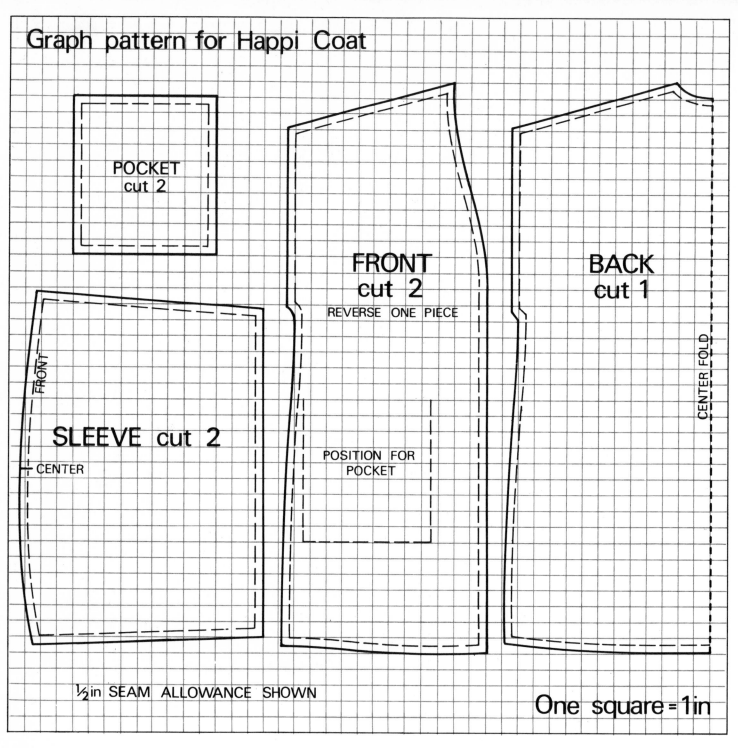

Graph pattern for Happi Coat

POCKET
cut 2

FRONT
cut 2
REVERSE ONE PIECE

POSITION FOR POCKET

BACK
cut 1

CENTER FOLD

SLEEVE cut 2

FRONT

CENTER

½in SEAM ALLOWANCE SHOWN

One square = 1in

together by making tiny hemming stitches round the curves of the second row of patches (figure 6).

Removing the backing papers

When all the patches are stitched together, press the work lightly on the wrong side. Snip the basting threads, pull them out, then remove the paper backing.

Lining patchwork

Patchwork is better lined, unless it is something small, such as a toy. Although patchwork is almost as durable as whole fabric, it is worthwhile extending the life of something into which you have put so much work.

Making the Happi coat

The Happi coat, in big, bright patchwork squares, makes an ideal housecoat or beach coat, and is fairly simple to make. Use cotton fabrics of equal weight for the patchwork, with facing fabric in one of the main colours of the patchwork.

You will need:

☐ A large bag of cotton fabric scraps in different colours and designs
☐ 2¾ yards unbleached dress weight calico, for lining
☐ 2¼ yards 36 inch wide navy cotton, for facings

Make a paper pattern from the graph (one square equals 1 inch) and, using

fabric scraps, cut patches approximately 4 inches by 4 inches (although some of the patches in the Happi coat illustrated are oblong). Lay the patchwork pieces out on a table until there are enough to make a Back, two Fronts, two Sleeves and two Pockets, seeing that colours are evenly distributed.

Keep the piles separate. Right sides facing, machine patches together into strips, allowing ½ inch seams throughout. Join strips to make the area of fabric required for each pattern piece.

For the sleeves, make two pieces of patchwork, each 22 inches by 15½ inches. For the back, make one piece, 35½ inches by 26 inches and, for the fronts, two pieces, each 36 inches by

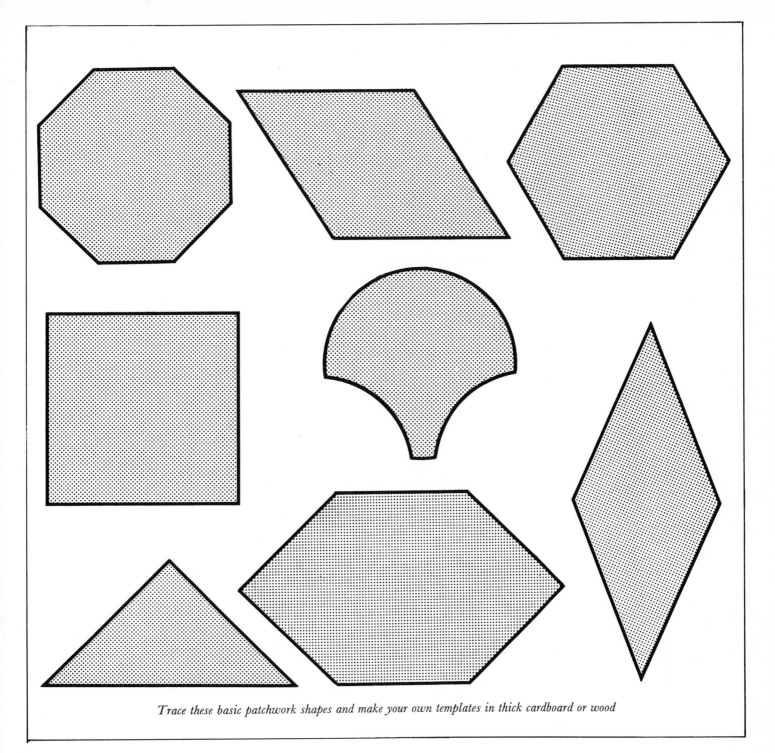

Trace these basic patchwork shapes and make your own templates in thick cardboard or wood

$12\frac{1}{2}$ inches. For the pockets, make two pieces, each 9 inches by $8\frac{1}{2}$ inches. Pin the pattern pieces to the patchwork and cut out one back on the fold, two sleeves, two fronts and two pockets. Pin the paper pattern pieces to the lining fabric and cut out the same pieces. Place one pocket lining against wrong side of one pocket, baste and sew by hand all around. Make the second pocket in the same way and then cut two pocket facings from the navy cotton fabric, each 9 inches by 4 inches. Place one facing edge to the upper edge of one pocket, baste and sew. Turn facing to inside, tuck raw edge under and stitch. Repeat with other pocket. Pin pockets to coat fronts in positions indicated on the graph. Baste and then machine stitch.

Baste the patchwork fronts to the lining fronts, wrong sides together. Baste and machine stitch the patchwork back only to the fronts along the shoulder seams and down the side seams, working on wrong side. Stitch back lining to shoulder seams and hem down side seams. Sew patchwork sleeve seams, with right side to inside, and then, right side to right side, ease sleeves into armholes and pin, baste and sew. Sew sleeve lining side seams, baste into sleeves, wrong side to wrong side, and hem to shoulder seam. Baste lining to patchwork all around the edges of the garment.

Facings

From navy cotton, cutting on the fold where it is convenient, cut one belt, 78 inches by 5 inches, two belt slots, each 3 inches by $2\frac{1}{2}$ inches, two front facings, each 39 inches by 4 inches, one hem, 52 inches by 5 inches, and two cuffs, each 21 inches by 5 inches. Make the belt slots and stitch in position at the waist.

Pin, baste and sew edge of facing to the edges of the coat, mitering hem and front facings neatly. Turn facings to wrong side, fold under the raw edges and hand sew to finish. Finish off cuffs in the same way.

Make the belt and pull through the belt slots.

Pattern names

Patchwork patterns, like recipes, have travelled from country to country acquiring local amendments and new names. America, a great country for patchwork since the first English and Dutch settlers brought the craft here, has such fascinating old names as Slave chain and Indian trail. Many patchwork names are descriptive — Ocean wave is lines of hexagons rising and falling in a zigzag, Windmill is triangles joined at a point, Dog's tooth a row of sharp triangles, and a pattern made of big and small stars is called Milky Way. Of single shapes, an equilateral hexagon is called a Honeycomb, a long hexagon a Church window, and coffin-shaped hexagon a Coffin. The liberal use of hexagons is characteristic of English work.

Patchwork for cushions

These two cushion designs use wider angled templates

Top cushion

The design has been carefully planned, using the border pattern in the fabric for the patches, to enhance the design on the cushion. This is where a perspex template or a 'window' gives you an advantage. The five eight-pointed star shapes are the ground material, where the patchwork has left an interesting shape in the middle. To fit this design on to a cushion 17in square, use $\frac{3}{4}$in octagon and square templates.

Bottom cushion

This is 17 inches square and has a design using $1\frac{1}{4}$in lozenge shapes. The interest is in the contrast between plain and patterned fabrics, as only one template shape was used.

How to make up

Join together the different patches to make up the design, baste round the outside edges and appliqué the patchwork to the ground material.

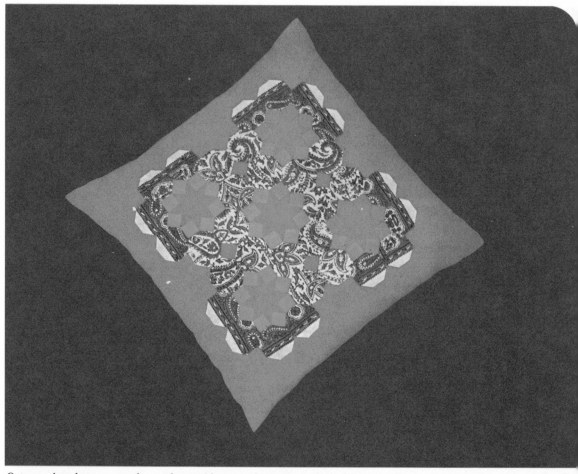

Octagonal and square patches make up this attractive pattern ▲ *·and lozenge shapes create an alternative design* ▼

Crazy patchwork

As the picture shows, this is patchwork built up in a truly random way, not only by the use of different materials but also by the total irregularity of the shapes. In many ways, this technique is closer to appliqué than patchwork as the different patches are stitched to a ground material and not to each other—the raw edges are turned under and the patches pinned behind each other on to the background. No papers are used for this method.

The advantage of crazy patchwork is that you can use any odd scraps of material which are too small to be used up in a geometric design.

To make crazy patchwork more interesting, some of the patches can be sewn on to the background with embroidery silk or metallic thread. Little sequins or pearls sewn into the center of a patch, or a cluster of beads on a rather plain material, also add life and variety to the work.

Rich crazy patchwork quilt►
▼ Detail of crazy patchwork

Preserving flowers

It doesn't matter whether you have a big garden or a small one, or even none at all, as long as you can get into the countryside there are masses of flowers, grasses, seed heads and leaves that can be picked and preserved for decorations.

A charming Victorian art revived, it is this easy accessibility of the basic materials which makes the craft so appealing.

Dried flowers have dozens of possibilities for decoration: preserved whole they make formal vase arrangements, table displays, wall plaques, and Christmas and party decorations. Pressed flat, they make charming collage pictures, table mats, book covers, book marks and greeting cards, to name but a few.

The choice of flowers

Gather flowers for preserving in the spring and summer, and for best results as soon as they have opened. If blossoms are too full blown, they are likely to either disintegrate or lose their colour. Flowers which will dry easily fall into two categories, the everlasting flowers such as Rodanthe and Acroclinium and others called 'soft flowers', some of which can be dried successfully if the process is quick. Here is a short list of flowers which can be preserved for whole flower decorations:

- Rodanthe: a small, deep red everlasting flower.
- Acroclinium: a rosy coloured annual everlasting flower.
- Statice sinuata: long stems of pink, mauve, violet, white and yellow.
- Statice limonium (sea lavender).
- Honesty: sometimes called 'silver pennies'.
- Chinese lanterns: orange lantern-like bracts.
- Cornflower: pink and blue.
- Love-in-the-mist: excellent for seed pods.
- Hydrangea: mature flower heads can be preserved.
- Delphiniums: blues, mauve and purple; small spikes preserve best, picked young.
- Golden rod: yellow gold spikes.
- Godetia: pink and red.
- Star of the Veldt: mixed colours.
- Marigolds: yellow and orange.
- Larkspur: pinks, mauve and purple.
- Sunflowers: double varieties of perennial types can be dried successfully.

Choosing for pressing

Almost any kind of flower can be gathered for pressing but it should be remembered that in pressing, bright colours will fade. Blues can fade to pale brown and bright red is likely to turn into chocolate

Dried grasses and preserved flowers are often at their most effective in casual profusion

▲ *A standing arrangement of dried flowers, grasses, ferns and poppy seed heads*

that some of the stems should be pressed in a curve for variety. Here is a list of grasses suitable for preserving:

☐ Briza maxima: nodding heads—ideal for Christmas decoration when glittered.
☐ Lagurus ovatus: (hare's tail grass)—like a squirrel's furry tail.
☐ Stipa pennata: (feather grass).
☐ Timothy grass

Leaves

Many wooded stemmed leaves such as beech, pittosporum, lime and laurel can be preserved on the branch by using a glycerine solution. Beech leaves are popular for this kind of preserving because the range of colours which can be achieved is so beautiful. The earlier branches of beech are cut, the deeper the colour will be after preserving. Branches gathered later will turn a light tan colour. Elaeagnus, camellia, box and many evergreens are also well worth preserving using the glycerine treatment.

For pressing purposes, tree leaves should not be picked when they are green because they fade. The colours of autumn foliage are beautiful and will keep their colours without fading, and fallen leaves can be collected, even if they are damp. Include the leaves of plants such as clematis and those with grey and silver colours, such as cineraria, diamond, artemisia, and absinthium in your collection. Raspberry leaves are grey on the underside and so is the gazania leaf, and the addition of these leaves to a collection is recommended.

Seedheads and berries

Some seedheads, collected while they are still green and unripe, can be successfully preserved by the glycerine method. Experiment with different kinds of flowers and plants to find out the colours and effects. Many are prettier left until they are ripe, and are preserved by drying—poppies, spiraea, delphiniums, columbines, for instance, and, of course, honesty. Chinese lanterns are gathered when the lower lanterns are just beginning to colour.

Some vegetables produce attractive seedheads for flower arrangements—parsley, fennel, onions and leeks, for example, as do many wild flowers and shrubs. Look for plants such as knapweed, types of cow parsley, dock, ripple-wort and teasles. Berries can be preserved, but for only a few weeks, by brushing them with a thin glue soon after they are picked.

Methods of preserving

Drying flowers

Wherever possible, cut flowers with long

brown, so make allowances for these changes when a pressed flower collection is being built up. Experiment with different kinds of petals and flowers and note the colour changes as they dry. Beautiful collage pictures can be made in tones of beige, pale browns, grey and silver white. Yellow flowers are good for pressing—buttercups, for instance, retain their colours for about a year—but even if flower petals are inclined to turn to tones of brown, their colours, combined with silvery leaves and autumn leaves, will give a wonderful colour range with which to work. Ideally, flowers should be picked

in the middle of the day when they are dry—try to avoid picking when damp.

Grasses

Grasses should be picked before they are fully mature to prevent their shedding seeds. A collection of grasses can therefore be started quite early in the summer and a good variety should be gathered, including some of the less decorative kinds. In whole flower arrangement, grass stems can be used for mounting flower heads and leaves, their flexible stems falling into pleasing curves quite naturally. Grasses can be pressed too, remembering

▲ *Hanging ornament using sycamore, barley ears and wild grass*

▲ *Hanging ornament using larch cones, ash and brome grass*

▲ *Thank-you card using flowers, ferns and seed heads*
▼ *Bookmark using flowers and birch leaves*

▲ *Matchbox top using buttercups, grasses, rush and vetch*
▼ *Table mat with a bird motif using leaves and honesty pod*

▲ Door finger plates using spring and summer flowers and mounted under glass

such as a shed or outhouse. The darker the better because light will turn the grasses into hay.

Preserving leaves
Split branch stems upwards for about two inches and immerse them immediately in warm water. Leave the branches for a few hours and discard any on which the leaves curl. Make a solution of one part glycerine to two parts hot water and insert the stems. As the stems only require two or three inches of solution, use a narrow vessel—a tin can for instance—for the preserving fluid, and stand the tin in a bucket so that the branches are supported. The leaves will 'turn' in about three weeks.

Stems
As the stems of some dried flowers turn brittle, the stem can be strengthened by inserting a piece of fine wire through the center of the flower, giving it a twist under the calyx. Alternatively, paint the stem just under the flower head with latex adhesive. This will dry stiff and clear and looks quite natural.

Natural looking false stems for flower heads and odd leaves are made with preserved grass stems—Timothy grass is particularly useful for supporting flower heads. Pierce the center of the flower with a match stick and thread the grass through, stem first, until the grass head touches the flower center. Trim the grass head off and pull it through a little more until it is almost invisible. Separate leaves can be attached to grass stems with a touch of latex adhesive.

Pressing flowers
Method 1. Pick the whole flower and place it as soon as possible between two sheets of blotting paper and then immediately between the pages of an old book which has absorbent paper pages. Several flowers can be arranged together on the sheets as long as they do not touch. When one sheet is complete, turn six or seven pages on in the book and proceed through until the book is full. Then place a heavy weight on the book—bricks or a flat iron will do, and leave it quite undisturbed for about four weeks. Do not look at the flowers at all while they are pressing. Leaving them quite undisturbed and the heavy weight on top is the secret of successful pressing.

Method 2. For flowers with a hard center or a hard formation, use a flower press.

Presses are often inclined to spoil delicate flowers and the book and brick method is better for these types of flowers.

stems. Tie into small bunches and hang heads downwards in a cool shady place with air circulation. It is important that the place be dry because damp conditions will make the flowers go mouldy, and if there is too much light the colours will fade. Some flowers, such as helichrysums, lose their heads when the stems are dried out. These can be mounted on false stems. An alternative method of drying whole flowers involves the use of powdered borax or Silica gel. Flowers dried in borax dry in about three weeks—only three days are required for flowers buried in Silica gel.

Method. Cover the bottom of a box or biscuit tin with the powder and then either lay flowers face down or stand them on their faces, depending on their structure. Pour more powder all over and round them, lifting the petals now and then, so that the flower is surrounded by powder but still retains its shape. Leave the flowers for the required time until they are brittle and dry. Take great care when removing the flowers from the powder.

Drying grasses
Tie grasses into tight bundles (they shrink during drying) and hang them heads downwards in a cool, dark place,

96

Pressing separate petals

In many cases, a far prettier effect in collage is achieved if petals are pulled off flowers for pressing and then reassembled when dried and pressed.

Decorations with whole flowers

Table arrangements using whole dried flowers can be made on a base of styrofoam or plasticine, but some of the easiest decorations to make with dried flowers and grasses are hanging ornaments. These are best made with a styrofoam center which is lightweight. Use a ball of styrofoam and tie it in halves and then quarters with coloured string or ribbon, leaving the ends for hanging. Fix a ribbon bow at the base with a long pin and then fill in the four quarters of the ball with dried flowers and seedheads. Should some of the flowers prove difficult to insert by their stems, pin them in place through the head of the flower into the foam.

Slightly more delicate in appearance are stars with cone centers, in which grasses or flower stalks are glued to the scales of a pine or larch-cone. Alternatively, a small cardboard disc can be used as a center, and with combinations of sycamore seeds, oat grains and dried flowers and grasses glued to both surfaces. Gilded or coloured, they make pretty Christmas decorations. Thistles can also be used as a base for hanging ornaments and so can hogweed, acorn-cups and yarrow-stalks.

Ideas using pressed flowers

Besides collage pictures, lovely accessories for the home and gifts can be made using pressed flowers. The finger plates illustrated in this chapter are a charming example.

To make finger plates, cut white cardboard to the size of a perspex finger plate and position the flowers and stalks. Stick the flowers down in the way described and cover with the perspex plate.

Matchboxes with a flower decorated top make acceptable gifts. Arrange small flowers and leaves on the lid of a large box previously covered with white paper and stick them down. Place a piece of adhesive plastic sheeting over the flowers, smoothing it down carefully. Once in position the adhesive plastic cannot be removed, and one should make sure that the flowers are firmly in position before applying it. Larger surfaces can be treated in the same way (notebooks, calendars and greeting cards, for example).

Another idea particularly suitable for the use of pressed flowers is a set of table

▲ *'Iceberg' flower collage. White rose petals were used for the two central flowers*

mats. Make them in sets, and to any dimensions, with a backing of colourful felt or tweed. The top surface of the mat is glass, cut to size by a glazier, in a 24oz or 32oz thickness which will resist the heat of all but the very hottest dinner plates. The edges of the mat are finally sealed with adhesive tape chosen in a colour that seems most suitable.

Collages with pressed flowers

Pressed flower collage is a most absorbing and creative craft, the petals, flower heads, stems, grasses and seeds forming an integral part of the composition itself. The theme of the collage may be more than a design of pressed flowers; it can become a picture, the shapes of leaves and flowers themselves providing the inspiration.

A latex based adhesive is best for sticking down flowers and petals. Choose one which is easily removed when it is rubbed off with a finger and leaves no stain on the paper. A soft paint brush is ideal for lifting petals and for arranging them in position. Tweezers are not recommended because they can damage the flowers. Always use adhesive sparingly in dried flower collage.

▲ This delightful beach basket and pair of summer sandals can be made from just over 1lb of raffia

Raffiawork

Raffia work, in the pleasing natural material, can be used to make any number of attractive and useful items, from tablemats to sandals. There are several different ways of using raffia; it makes a brilliant embroidery thread; it can be wound and woven over a cardboard base, it can be woven to produce a piece of fabric. It can also be coiled and twisted around thick sisal string to make a really firm structure, such as the beach basket shown here. Raffia work is a fascinating craft—and it's ideal to take away for something to do on holiday—light, easy to carry, and very relaxing once you've mastered the basic techniques. You could start by making tablemats in easy single and double stitch, and go on to make our basket and sandals.

Raffia, the immature leaf of the African palm, comes mostly from Malagasy and natural, dry raffia is essential for this kind of work. Prepared raffia is glycerined and the moisture it contains reduces the tautness of the finished work, making it look and feel limp. Natural raffia is sold in hanks of varying sizes, and is bought by the pound weight.

For the beginner, sisal string is the best foundation on which to coil the raffia—3-ply is a good thickness. Cane of the cheapest quality can be used in place of sisal, but if it is used, do not soak it with water as you would for cane work.

It is important that the hairs of the sisal do not show through between the raffia coils; they should be smoothed down during working and the sisal string can be pulled through a piece of beeswax first, which will help to keep the hairs down. If a few do show when the work is finished, they can be cut off, but it would be a long, tedious job to cut off many.

Tools

A needle with a large eye and a blunt point (a No. 14 tapestry needle is ideal) and a pair of scissors are all the tools needed for raffia work.

Methods of working

Begin by working a coil for the foundation row.

Cut sisal string diagonally for about 1 inch, making a kind of point to reduce thickness in the finished join when the end is tucked in. Run string through beeswax, to reduce the number of hairs that stand up. Thread needle with enough strands of raffia to equal the thickness of one ply of the sisal string.

Using your left forefinger and thumb, hold both the cut end of sisal string and one end of the raffia, leaving the other end of raffia, with the needle attached, hanging free (diagram 1).

With the right forefinger and thumb, hold only the raffia, still leaving needle hanging free. The raffia, now held with the right forefinger and thumb, is in position to coil on to the sisal string to make the foundation row (referred to from now on as 'the row below') (diagram 2).

To do this, proceed as follows:

Using your right forefinger and thumb, twist the raffia evenly for about 1 inch, then coil that twisted raffia, working away from you, around the sisal string, as if you were turning the handle of a sewing machine. Thus you will get a good, even tension. Twist another inch of raffia and coil that around, keeping the raffia taut all the time to stop it unwinding. Continue covering the sisal string with twisted raffia, bending the string to form a circle.

To join

Tuck the end of the sisal into the first one or two coils and resume coiling until the whole ring is completely covered (diagram 3).

The foundation row or the 'row below' is now completely covered with twisted raffia. Continue to cover the sisal string with the twisted raffia for six or eight coils; this is the beginning of your second circle. You can continue to work in circles, to make a tablemat, as shown in diagrams 4 and 5, in which single and double stitches are used.

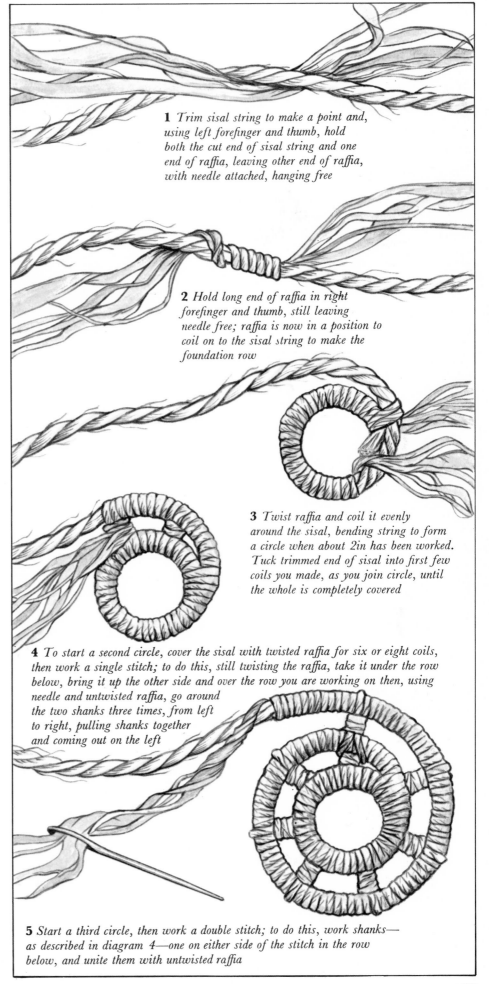

1 *Trim sisal string to make a point and, using left forefinger and thumb, hold both the cut end of sisal string and one end of raffia, leaving other end of raffia, with needle attached, hanging free*

2 *Hold long end of raffia in right forefinger and thumb, still leaving needle free; raffia is now in a position to coil on to the sisal string to make the foundation row*

3 *Twist raffia and coil it evenly around the sisal, bending string to form a circle when about 2in has been worked. Tuck trimmed end of sisal into first few coils you made, as you join circle, until the whole is completely covered*

4 *To start a second circle, cover the sisal with twisted raffia for six or eight coils, then work a single stitch; to do this, still twisting the raffia, take it under the row below, bring it up the other side and over the row you are working on then, using needle and untwisted raffia, go around the two shanks three times, from left to right, pulling shanks together and coming out on the left*

5 *Start a third circle, then work a double stitch; to do this, work shanks—as described in diagram 4—one on either side of the stitch in the row below, and unite them with untwisted raffia*

Single stitch

To make a single stitch for connecting your second row to your first row, still twisting the raffia, take it into the row below, bring it up to the other side and over the row you have started to work. The needle now comes into use for uniting the two shanks of raffia.

Take the raffia (not twisted) and the needle around the two shanks, from left to right, pulling shanks tightly together so they meet. Meanwhile, with the left forefinger and thumb, hold the row you are working and the row below, so that a flat shape is achieved. Go round the shanks twice more with untwisted raffia. Be sure always to come out on the left-hand side, so the work will look the same on both sides.

Double Stitch

This is made by forming shanks, as for the single stitch, one on either side of the stitch in the row below, and then united by untwisted raffia.

Treble Stitch

To form a treble stitch, the row below must have two stitches close together. Make the shanks of the first stitch to the right of the two stitches below; make the second between the two stitches, and the third on the left of the two stitches. Unite these three shanks as the double stitch, using untwisted raffia.

When you have mastered these basic stitches, you will be able to design your own work, or make our beach basket and sandals.

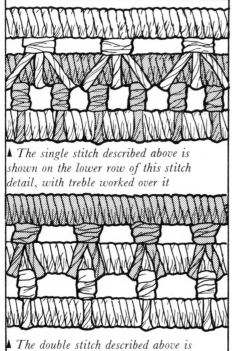

▲ *The single stitch described above is shown on the lower row of this stitch detail, with treble worked over it*

▲ *The double stitch described above is shown on the top row of this stitch detail, with single stitches worked on the row below*

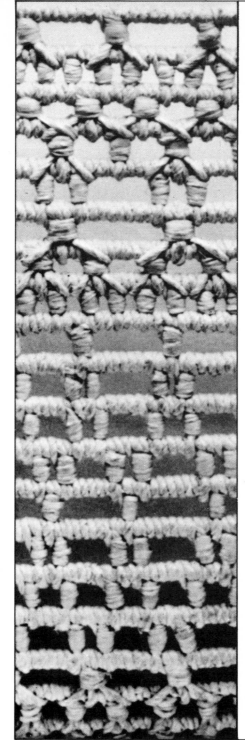

For the basket sides, work as follows:
1st row: Work single stitches into the fillis string, working 7 stitches to every 3in ∗
2nd row: Work one double stitch into each single stitch in row below
3rd row: Work one treble stitch into each two double stitches below
4th row: Work single stitches into row below, two stitches over each treble
5th row: Work in single stitch, one stitch to either side of two single stitches in row below
6th row: Work two single stitches inside every two stitches in row below
7th row: Work one single stitch between each two in row below
8th row: Work one single stitch either side of single stitches in row below
9th row: Work two single stitches between groups of two stitches in row below
10th row: Work single stitches in groups of two between groups of two in row below
11th row: Work one single stitch into centre of each two in row below
12th row: Work three single stitches between each stitch in row below
13th row: Work one treble stitch over every two stitches in row below
14th row: Work one treble over every two treble stitches in row below
15th row: Work one single stitch either side of each treble in row below
16th row: Work one treble over each two singles in row below, and one single between each treble
17th row: Work two trebles over every three trebles in row below
18th row: Work two singles between each treble of row below
19th row: Work one double stitch over two single stitches in row below, leaving one single stitch free between each double
Now work handles: instructions are given right ∗

Beach basket

You will need
- ☐ 1 lb natural, dry raffia
- ☐ Sisal string
- ☐ Beeswax
- ☐ One hank of fillis or soft white garden string
- ☐ 2 No. 12 or 14 tapestry needles
- ☐ Scissors
- ☐ A plywood basket base, ready bored, available in different shapes and sizes

To prepare the basket base
Using fillis string and the two tapes-

try needles, thread string both ways through each hole on plywood base, threading needles and string opposite ways through one hole and working all the way around, so both sides of plywood are completely threaded. Finish by tying a neat knot on the one side and work on this side, so the raffia work hides the knot.

Working the pattern
Follow the detail photograph of the basket's side for the pattern but, if you prefer, work out a random pattern of your own. Our basket measures approx-

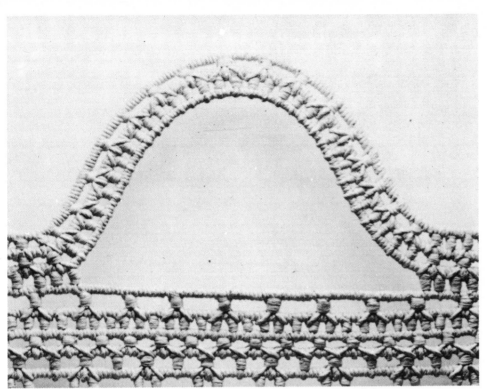

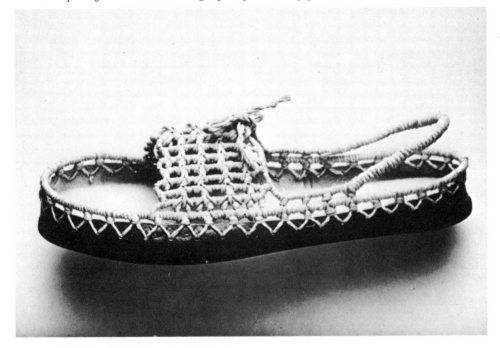

▲ *A detail of the basket handles, for which full instructions are given, below*
▼ *Make a pair of sandals to this design quickly and easily from the instructions, right*

imately 9 inches deep by 19½ inches wide.

The handles

When the sides have been worked, mark out a space 7 inches wide in the center of the top row on both sides, using pieces of contrast thread.

Work a row of single stitches into the row below, working three single stitches to 1 inch, starting from one left-hand piece of marker thread and working around to the opposite marker thread on the other side of basket.

Wind twisted raffia around the sisal for 11½ inches and then, leaving this 11½ inches free for the handle, work single stitches into row below, exactly as before. When the marker thread on the opposite side is reached, wind twisted raffia around sisal for 11½ inches and then work a row of treble stitch, making 3 treble stitches to every 2 inches all around basket, working each treble stitch over two shanks of the row below. When the prepared handle sections are reached, work single stitches. Work a final row, working single stitches between double stitches: 3 double stitches and 2 single stitches to 1 inch. Work treble stitches over handles.

Sandals

You will need
☐ ½oz natural dry raffia
☐ Sisal string
☐ Beeswax
☐ Pair of moccasin bases, ready bored
☐ No 12 or 14 tapestry needle
☐ Scissors

Work a row of double stitches into all the holes on the moccasin bases, working right shank of a stitch into same hole as left shank of last stitch made, for the welt. Place your foot into moccasin and mark where the heel strap is to join to main part of sandal and where the uppers are to be placed.

Left foot
Starting on outside left of the welt where the upper begins, nearest the toes, work towards heel, as follows:
1st row: 8 single stitches, for 2¾ inches, then bend sisal back towards toe, as shown in the illustration.
2nd row: Work 1 double stitch, 3 treble stitches and 1 double.
3rd row: bend sisal back towards heel and work 1 single and 4 double stitches.
4th row: Bending sisal towards toe again, work a row of five double stitches.
5th row: Bending sisal back over work, make 1 single and 4 double stitches.
6th row: Bending sisal, work 1 single and 4 double stitches.
7th row: Bending sisal, work 1 single and 4 double stitches.
Bending sisal over outside edge of heel side of upper, work a single stitch into top end loop, then a double stitch into top end loop and second loop, then a single stitch into second loop, and a single into third loop of flap. Make four double stitches into side of sandal, having by this time gone around back edge of flap. When first heel strap position is reached, make a thick coil, using sisal and raffia, joining again with another double at the other heel strap position. Work other side of upper in the same way.
Make right foot sandal to match.
Plait two strands of raffia for ties, thread them through the holes and then knot the ends to secure.

Both the sandals and the basket can be worked in different coloured strands of raffia, to give an exciting contrast. Natural coloured raffia can be dyed at home, using any ordinary household boiling dye. This produces lovely pastel shades which are fast dyed. Try the sandal ties in two colours and natural— red and blue, perhaps—for a trim.

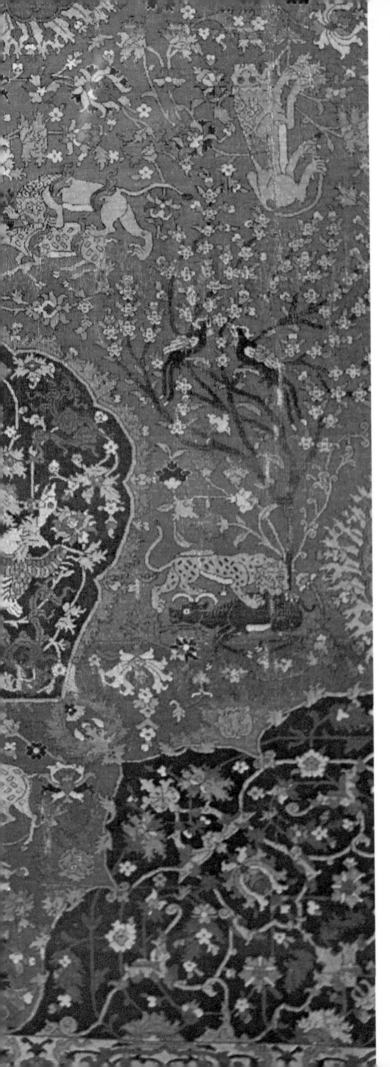

Rugs

When digging your toes into a cosy rug by the fire have you ever longed to be able to make one for yourself? Well, here, with the help of this book you can learn how to do it.

We explain clearly the stages involved in making a number of rugs in a variety of yarns that include luxurious, thick piled carpets and shaggy multi-coloured Rya rugs, all made with a simple latchet hook. The techniques achieve maximum effect at minimum cost and remember, men have been known to enjoy rug-making too, so see of you can get them to join in.

Hooked rugs

Using cut wool with a latchet hook is one of the easiest and fastest ways of making a rug. The straightforward technique produces a warm, hard-wearing, thick pile that will last for a lifetime. There are three ways you can set about making a pile rug. You can buy a kit with the design already printed onto the canvas, with the correct amounts of wool in each colour included: you can buy plain canvas with a charted design and you choose your own colour scheme, or, if you are adventurous, you can just buy a strip of canvas and make up a design of your own.

What you will need to design your own rug

Canvas: this comes in various widths from 12in to 48in, so there is plenty of choice for whatever size of rug you make. A good size for a hearth or bedside rug is 6ft by 3ft. The canvas you need is 10 holes to 3in rug canvas and is usually divided up with either red or brown threads making squares, 3 inches by 3 inches ten holes by ten holes.

Wool: the correct wool for hooked rugs is a coarse 6ply rug wool. This is available either in skeins, which can be cut to whatever length you want by winding the wool round a grooved wooden gauge and then slicing along the groove with a sharp razor blade, or you can buy it pre-cut in bundles of 320 pieces. These are called units and one unit will cover 3 squares. For the oversewn edge, buy skeins of wool to match.

Tools: a latchet-hook is the only tool you will need and it is available from any handicraft shop. Shaped like a large crochet hook with a wooden handle, it has a hinged latchet which closes the open end of the hook as you make the rug knot, and prevents the canvas from becoming entangled.

The technique of carpet and rug making was perfected by the Persians and this, the Chelsea carpet, is a superb example

How to start

Lay your canvas on a table with the full length stretching away from you. A good plan is to secure it with a heavy weight or a pile of books at the other end. Then, to prevent the cut ends from fraying, fold the end of the canvas over for about two inches (frayed edge uppermost) exactly matching each hole with the hole beneath. It makes the rug easier to work if you baste this in position. Now work the first few rows of knots through this double thickness, so losing the rough ends in the pile of the rug.

To make a really hard-wearing rug finish it with an oversewing stitch round the edges. There are several methods for doing this (see pages 106–107).

Leave the outside thread of canvas free and one square at either side next to the selvage so that they can be oversewn at the end. Start working the rug from left to right, (right to left if you are left handed) and keep working in parallel rows. Don't be tempted to do patches of the pattern and then join them up as this will give a very uneven finished appearance and also, with the thick wool, it is easy to miss squares.

Ways to use rugs

Rugs don't just have to live on floors. In central Asia, rugs were used as decorative wall hangings, so perhaps if you have a bare wall a colourful rug would make an interesting new texture in the room. Alternatively you could make a long narrow rug and hang it with big rings to make a cosy backing for a bed settee.

A very simple design using a combination of colours in stripes ▼

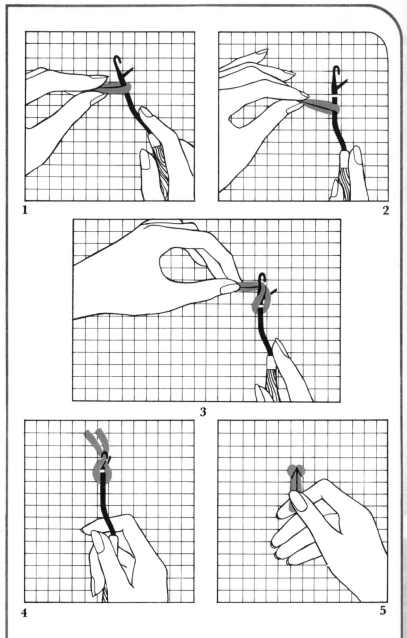

The 4 movement knot

There are two methods of making the knots in a hooked rug—the 4 movement method featured here is just quicker than the 5 movement method (see page 108).

The difference is the way the knots lie which effects the direction of the pile. By using both methods two people can work on a rug at the same time—one at each end—and when they finally meet in the middle, the pile will be lying in the same direction.

1. Fold cut length of wool in half and holding it between the thumb and index finger of the left hand, loop it around the neck of the latchet-hook.

2. Still holding onto the ends of the wool, insert the hook under the first of the horizontal (weft) threads.

3. Turning the hook a little to the right, take the ends of the wool around the hook.

4. Pull the latchet-hook under the weft thread and through the loop of wool, catching the two ends in the hook as the latchet closes automatically.

5. Pull the ends of the wool tight to check that the knot is firm. The tuft will finish up lying towards you.

A sunflower rug

Plotting the design of a rug from a chart on to the canvas needs care. For complicated designs, such as Oriental patterns, it is easiest to buy a canvas already stencilled with the pattern. If you plot your own pattern, remember that it will show the colour of the stitches in the holes, whereas the actual stitches are worked on the lines of the canvas.

How to work from a chart

If you are using a chart, it makes it easier if you first mark the design on to the canvas with a felt pen. Draw a vertical line down the center of the canvas from which to work the pattern. To mark the base of the stalk, count 6 rows up from the bottom of the canvas (after folding over a hem of 1½in), and mark the 2 middle

holes, that is, the ones immediately on either side of the center line. Then, following the chart, count up the holes and mark the design on the canvas. It will simplify later work if the colour changes on the chart are marked with a corresponding felt pen on the canvas.

Once you have grasped the basic idea of the pattern, you can alter it to fit your own canvas. One flower, two leaves and a stalk take 1,018 holes, and 4 units. Work out the total number of holes in the canvas (width holes multiplied by length holes) and subtract from it the number of holes for each flower or flowers. The resulting background number, divided by 320, will give you the number of wool units you need in the background colour. The main thing is to subtract from the total number of holes however many flowers you decide to work on to your canvas.

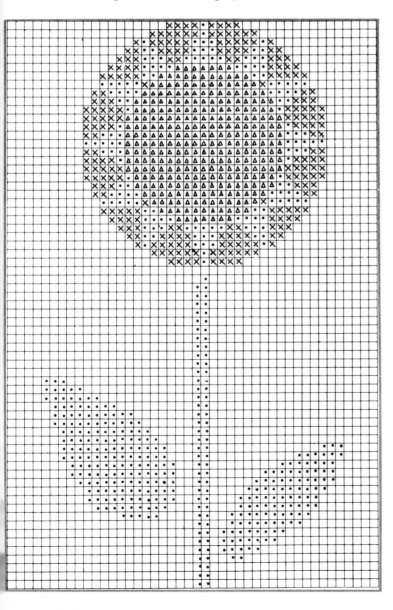

▲ *Ideas for rugs using general sunflower motifs*

The sunflower rug

This sunflower rug is about 24in by 24in and you can use it as a wall picture or backed, and filled, as a floor cushion.
Working on the quantities suggested on page 103 you will need:
☐ Canvas 24in wide, 27in long: (24in is a standard width with selvages, 27in allows an extra 1½in at each end to turn over).
☐ Yarn total 6,400 holes (80 x 80)
    red—1 unit (231 holes)
    yellow—1 unit (294 holes)
    green—2 units (493 holes)
    cream—17 units (5,382 holes)
    ie, each flower with its leaves and stalk
    needs 4 units of wool to cover 1,018 holes
☐ One latchet hook
☐ Extra cream rug wool in a skein, not cut, for binding the edges of the finished rug (see pages 106–107).
☐ Rug needle

Fringes and finishes

A lot of work goes into a rug and it is meant to take a lot of wear and tear, especially at the edges. Knowing how to finish and strengthen these edges correctly will do more than anything' to preserve a rug's good looks. Otherwise, the outside tufts soon tend to lie down and the selvages quickly begin to wear away. Cut lengths of yarn are only used for the tufts of a rug—for finishing the edges you will need skeins of matching rug yarn. If a rug, or part of a rug, has already been worked, it is still possible to finish the edges at a later stage as long as one hole of rug canvas has been left free on each side for turning in the selvages. If you are just beginning to work a rug with a patterned design, play safe by working the edging stitch along one end only and up part of the sides. Make sure that the pattern will be symmetrical and quite complete before you finish the other edges. If you don't, you may have the frustrating task of picking the work apart to correct any miscalculations. Two special edging stitch methods are covered in this chapter, one worked with a needle and one with a crochet hook, as well as an attractive fringed finish—just choose the one you think is most suitable for your particular rug.

Plaited stitch method

Of the several stitches you can use to finish the edges securely, plaited stitch is usually the best one. It is simple and quick to do and, at the same time, is attractive to look at. Incidentally, it is easy to repair whenever accidents or wear and tear take their toll. Plaited stitch is just as suitable for finishing the needle-made rugs described in later chapters.

How to work plaited stitch

This stitch is worked from right to left. Work with the cut edge folded uppermost overlapping about five holes, and the selvages turned in tightly, so that you sew over only half their width.
1. Bring the needle through from the back of the canvas, leaving about three inches of yarn as a tail lying along the top edge where it can be held by your left hand. This will be covered by the stitches as you go along. Then, take the needle over the edge to the back again and bring it through one hole to the left.
2. Take the needle over the edge and back through the first hole.
3. Take the needle over the edge again and bring it from back to front through the third hole to the left. Take it over the edge for the final time and bring it through the second hole to the right. Continue, moving forward three holes and back two, remembering that the needle should always pass from the back to the front of the canvas. On reaching the left-hand corner go back two, forward two, back one, forward one, and then continue around the selvage, starting again with step 1.

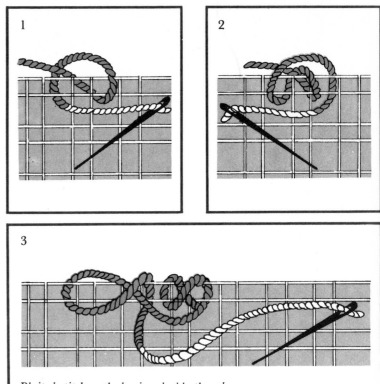

Plaited stitch method using double-thread canvas

The crochet edging stitch

Use a No. J crochet hook. Fold over the cut edges of your canvas and selvages as for plaited stitch.
Work from right to left.
1. Push the crochet hook through the first hole and pull back a loop of yarn, leaving a long tail which you can darn in afterward.
2. With the loop still on the crochet hook, catch the yarn from the back over the top of the canvas and pull it through the loop.
3. Put the crochet hook through the next hole and catch the yarn from the back and pull it through the hole.
4. Then catching the yarn again from over the top, pull it through the two loops already on the hook.
5. Push the hook through the third hole and continue repeating steps 3 and 4. To join the yarn, always leave a long end from your first ball and from the new ball to darn in afterward.

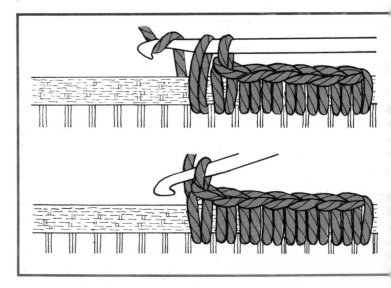

A hooked, Persian-style rug with plaited stitch edging

Attractive cotton fringe, using three strands of cotton for each tassel

Fringing

Fringing is always attractive and helps to add extra inches to the length of your rug. Originally this was the cut and knotted warp threads from a rug woven on a loom, but there is a quick and easy way to add a fringe to your canvas foundation and you can vary the colours as you feel. Cotton thread is sturdy and gives your rug a professional look.

How to make a fringe

It is really easier to add the fringing when you have completed the rug. Hook it as already described, turning in the rough ends and working an edging stitch up the sides as you go. For the fringing prepare lengths of cotton thread according to the width of fringe you want, remembering that the threads will be only half as long when they are knotted in the fringe.

Place the rug across a table and secure it with a weight. Then facing the shorter side of the rug, work from left to right using a latchet-hook. Insert the hook under the first canvas thread. Loop the group of cotton threads around the hook holding the ends between your thumb and index finger of the left hand as for the four-movement hooking method.

Pull the hook back under the horizontal thread and then pushing it forward through the loop, catch the ends in the latchet and bring them back to form a knot. Pull tight to secure.

When you have finished one end of the rug, brush the ends towards you and trim any longer threads to make it even. Steam the fringe to straighten it.

How to make a Rya rug

Rya means shaggy. Because the density of its pile is good insulation against the cold winters the rya is found all over Scandinavia. Originally ryas were woven on a loom with the pile knotted on the warp threads by hand but now you can use a canvas foundation and knot the wool with a latchet hook. The close-up shows the twisted wool, shaggy pile and subtle mingling of colours.

Colour blended ryas

Rya rugs have an individual style of colouring. Each knot is made of three strands of wool which allows enormous scope for using different shades of colour to build up a rich texture. A colourful rya rug makes an attractive and very cosy addition to your home whether you use it formally on the floor or hung on the wall. A rya floor cushion is quick to make and, as an introduction to the technique, gives a good idea of the versatility of this method of rug making. The cushion can be made any size—24in square makes a comfortable seat and is not too big to move about easily.

Materials
The canvas to use has 10 squares to 3in and the most suitable wool is a twisted 2 ply coarse rug wool which comes in 25 gramme skeins (4 skeins to a hank). Each skein makes approximately 56 knots.

Cutting the skeins
After buying the canvas, wool and latchet-hook cut the skeins into pieces the correct length for working. Unravel the skein of wool and holding it fully extended, cut cleanly through the two ends. Then fold these lengths in half and cut again, halve and cut once more. The skein is now divided into eight and you have a pile of cut threads. (It's a good idea to keep the different coloured cut wools in separate polythene bags.) If the cut lengths seem a bit irregular don't bother to trim them as the general look of the rug is shaggy.

Working a rya
Turn in the rough ends as for the thick pile rugs and start to hook in the tufts from left to right (right to left if you are left handed) using three strands of wool in each knot. If you are making a rug remember to work an edging stitch along one end and partly up both sides before you start. This isn't necessary for a floor cushion as you will be sewing it to a backing, but leave the first and last threads free along the turned in ends.

With skeins of closely related colours rather than complete contrasts you can grade the colours as you wish, increasing or decreasing a colour to get the required intensity or softness. Hook every alternate row, that is, leave one horizontal thread of canvas free between each row of knots.

Backing a floor cushion
When completed the cushion will need backing with a sturdy upholstery material as this is the side that will be getting the most wear. Choose a colour that blends with the colours you have used for the rya top.

Cut a square of backing material ¾in larger than the size of the worked canvas. Put the two right sides together pinning them firmly. Stitch through from the canvas side. On the selvage stab stitch through to the backing catching each thread of canvas inside the selvage. Hem the other two edges catching the outside thread of each hole. Leave one side open, turn inside out and stuff the cushion with either two old pillows or a 24in cushion pad available through most soft furnishing stores.

5-movement Latchet-hook method

The second method for hooking both short pile and rya rugs is the 5-movement method. The 4-movement method was shown on page 104 where it was explained that using the two methods two people can knot a rug—one at each end—at the same time.

1. Turn up the frayed end of the canvas as before and insert the latchet-hook under the first of the horizontal (weft) threads.

2. Hold the two ends of the piece of wool with your left hand and loop it over the hook.

3. Pull the hook back through the canvas until the wool loop is halfway through the hole, then push the hook through the loop until the latchet is clear.

4. Turn the latchet-hook, place the cut ends in the crook and pull the hook back through the loop. The latchet closes automatically.

5. Be sure to pull the knot tight.

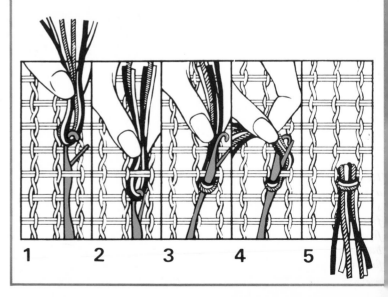

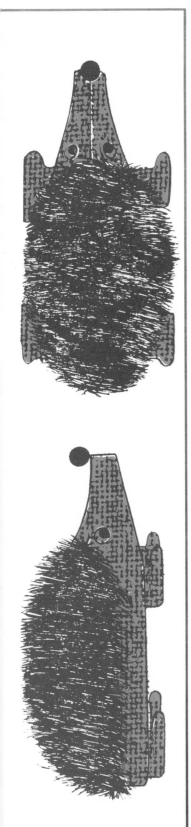

Here's an idea for the nursery—a large, cuddly hedgehog which is soft enough to sit on. Make him from burlap, stuff with kapok or foam, and then work a shaggy rya back. Also shown on this page is a fine example of a real rya rug.

Leatherwork

New approach to leathercraft

One of the oldest of crafts, leather work fell into obscurity at the end of the nineteen-thirties, when pride in craftsmanship gave way to mass production. Thonging, as a means of joining two pieces of leather, was out, and fashion demanded that craftmanship did not show, and that the article bore as close a resemblance to the machine-made as was possible.

A gayer, livelier interpretation of the original craft has now developed, losing none of the old standards yet making use of modern techniques. The essence of current fashion is reflected in the choice of materials and colours, and the way in which designers are now using suede and leather shows an exciting awareness of the scope of natural fibres.

To be able to design and make exciting and luxurious looking garments and accessories in leather and suede, it is important to know a little about the different kinds of leather and the best uses for them.

Different kinds of leather

For most of the makes a beginner will want to attempt, sheep skin is probably the best skin to use. It is supple, easily obtainable and falls into the medium price bracket. Sheep skin is dyed to a wide variety of colours as well as being finished in attractive natural tones, and can be used for leather garments and is ideal for accessories. Sheep skin suede is of a particularly good quality, soft and velvety, and is usually used for better quality fashion clothes.

Cowhide is a much heavier leather and comes in two or three different thicknesses, the central area of the hide being the thickest. This is used for shoe soles, suitcases and anything which needs to wear well. The sides of these hides are thinner and are suitable for heavier weight garments, such as skirts and jerkins and shoe uppers.

Cowhide is also sold in 'splits', which means that the skin has been split through its thickness into two layers. Splits are the cheapest kind of leather to buy, but are not terribly strong and shouldn't be used for articles where there is likely to be a strain on the leather—such as across the shoulders of a garment. It's perfectly suitable for accessories and is easily obtainable.

Calfskin, the smooth, beautiful leather used for good handbags and shoes, is available in different weights and finishes and is more expensive than sheepskin.

Among the fancy leathers are pigskins, goatskins, lizard and snake skin and fish skin, but these are generally rather difficult to obtain.

Leather and suede is sold by the square foot unless one is buying offcuts or scrap pieces. Skins are of an irregular shape with the legs and neck of the animal sticking out from the 'body', but these are calculated in the given measurement.

The basic tools

To make even quite simple things, a few basic tools are essential. The most important are a cutting board, a sharp leather knife and a good pair of scissors; ideally

This impressive jerkin is deceptive, being easy and cheap to assemble from odd scraps of leather and suede

these should be leather shears but this isn't essential. A bone folder, which nowadays is sometimes made of plastic, is used for scoring lines on the leather and for smoothing and flattening edges. A skiving knife, available from craft shops, is invaluable where hems and turnings need to be as thin as possible. Useful adjuncts are an oilstone on which to keep the knife sharp, a leather punch for thonged articles, a stitch marking wheel and a stitch tool, which makes slits for the thread instead of holes. A steel ruler, a set square and a compass are necessary for accurate measuring.

Sewing leather and suede

Of the four basic methods of joining leather—glueing, lacing or thonging, machine stitching and hand sewing—the latter two are used most.

To sew leather by hand, both straight and curved needles, glovers needles (which have a sharp triangular point) and saddlers needles are used, depending on the item being stitched.

For sewing using a sewing machine, medium thick needles will be found to be the most satisfactory, and the size of stitch should be regulated to the thickness of the leather. For thick work, set the stitch large, and for fine leather the stitch can be relatively small. Suedes tend to drag when more than one thickness is going through the machine, and to correct this adjust the stitch to the next size up. The thread will sink into the suede anyway and the finished appearance should be satisfactory.

Threads for leathercraft

Choose a thread suitable for the job in hand, determining the gauge for both appearance and performance. Whichever thread is chosen however, it must be waxed with beeswax or paraffin wax before use to prevent fraying and breaking. Heavier kinds of cotton, silk and nylon threads can be used for hand sewing and for machine stitching, providing that the machine needle is the right size. Linen thread is both decorative and strong for hand sewing and is ideal for thin, supple leathers and suedes. Buttonhole silk is appropriate for gloves and bags, while bookbinders thread and carpet yarn, available in different gauges, are very strong and are suitable for most types of leather. Saddler's thread is good for heavy duty articles.

Preparing leather for joining.

Sewing leather by hand can be fairly hard work, and by piecing holes first the job is made much easier. For saddlestitch-

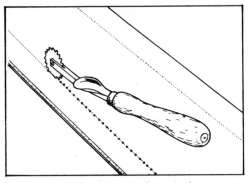

1. *Piercing with stitch marking wheel*

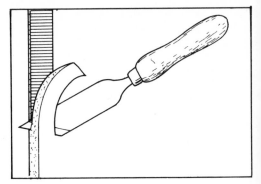

2. *The technique of skiving*

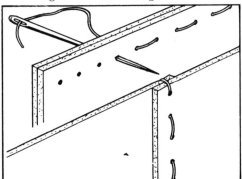

3. *Working running stitch*

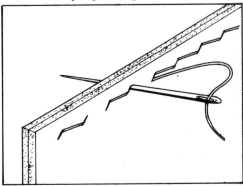

4. *Double running stitch*

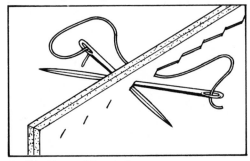

5. *Working saddle stitch*

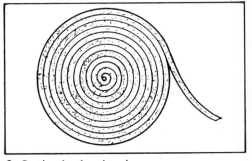

6. *Cutting leather thonging*

ing, pierce the holes with a sharp pointed awl but make sure that the holes are equidistant. Pierce along a ruler's edge or use a stitch marking wheel (diagram 1).

For leather and suedes which aren't too heavy, use the sewing machine without thread in the needle to pierce holes.

For lacing or thonging, holes are either punched or slit. Slit punches and pronged thonging tools can be purchased in craft shops; a plier-action punch is best for making round holes.

Skiving. Skiving is the term used for paring down the edges of leather and suede so that they can be more easily turned for glueing. Diagram 2 shows the technique. The knife is held at a very tight angle against the wrong side of the leather and guided towards the body and outwards.

Stitching seams by hand

There are three methods of stitching seams by hand, these are:

Running stitch. This is used for joining

ordinary seams and lapped seams. If thongs are being used for stitching, punch holes first in the leather. On lightweight leathers and suedes sew with a glovers needle. For heavier leathers, pierce holes and sew with a saddler's needle (diagram 3).

Double running stitch. This gives a much stronger join and has something of the appearance of saddle stitching. Sew the seam once, using a gloving needle and a single running stitch. Then sew back the other way using an ordinary needle. The change of needles is necessary because if a gloving needle were used for the second stitching, the spear-like point would cut the first stitches (diagram 4).

Saddle stitching. For this attractive finish, first wax the thread. Beeswax is used by professional workers but paraffin candle wax will do quite well. Pierce holes at a slight angle and then work as shown in diagram 5. Two needles are used simultaneously to pull threads through and it is important to make uniform stitches.

▲ *This beautiful patent leather clutch bag can also be made in soft calf or suede*

Thonging and lacing

Leather thonging can be purchased but it is quite easy to cut one's own. Diagram 6 shows the method.

Glueing

There are good leather glues available in craft shops in both tubes and jars. Tubes are useful for edges and small areas; a jar with a brush is more satisfactory for larger areas. Rubber solution and latex based adhesives are good because they will rub off without leaving a stain.

Glueing is mostly used for attaching lining leathers to surface leathers and for putting on decorative leather edgings and bindings.

Making a clutch bag

Patent leather has been used to make the bag illustrated, but any kind of leather or suede can be used instead. The pattern is based on very simple principles and can be adapted to make a coin purse, a tobacco pouch or even, if it were enlarged,

a simple brief case.

Copy the diagram onto squared paper. Decide whether you are going to skive the edges so that they can be turned in for the same finish as the bag illustrated. If you decide not to attempt this kind of finish, the edges can be left raw. The line for cutting leather for a raw edged finish is coloured.

When the pattern is outlined on the squared paper cut out the pieces, main bag and gussets, in heavy paper and take these with you to a leather supplier to choose a skin. Choose a lining skin, called a 'skiver' at the same time.

Cutting out

Lay the pattern pieces on the skin so that the best area of leather is used for the flap. The paper pattern can be kept in position by sticking it to the leather with one or two pieces of sticky tape. Mark round the pattern carefully with a pencil using a ruler. It is worth stressing at this point that making up difficulties will be

minimised if three rules are observed:
1. cut out the paper pattern carefully;
2. mark the pattern carefully on the skin;
3. be really accurate in cutting out the leather.

Skive the edges of the leather at this point if this is the technique you are following.

Interlining and pocket

Cut three pieces of card interlining to the measurements given on the diagram and glue them to the wrong side of the leather, making sure that the edges are absolutely parallel. This is important if the bag is to fold properly. If a fastening is being used this is the point at which the plates of the fastening are inserted. Press studs can be used instead if preferred. Turn the skived edges of the bag flap and front edge (A-B-C-D and F-G in the diagram). Snip into the turnings ½ inch where the top edge of the gusset will lie (D-d and A-a). Turn in and stick down the top edges of the gusset pieces too. Leave to dry.

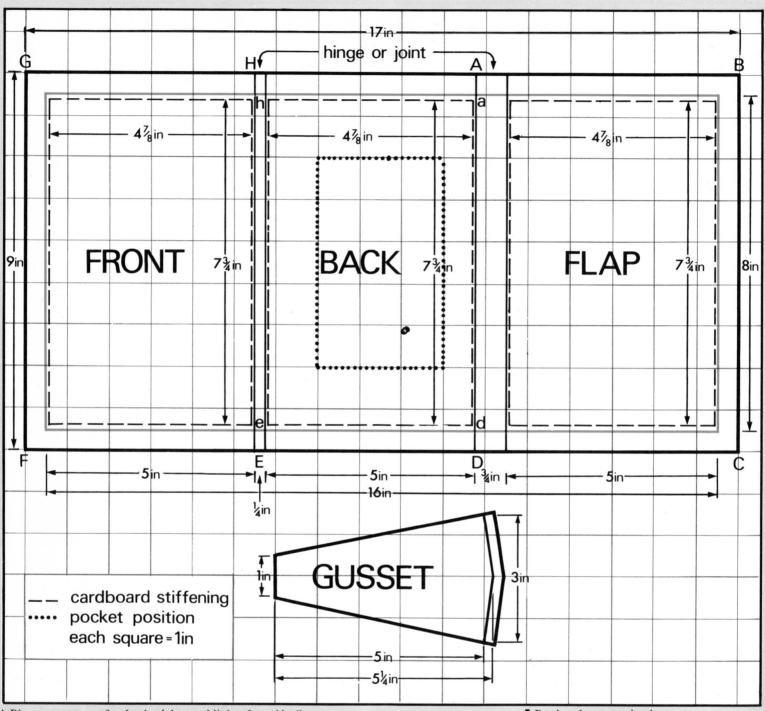

17in

hinge or joint

G   H   A   B

4⅞in   4⅞in   4⅞in

h   a

FRONT   7¾in   BACK   7¾in   FLAP   7¾in

9in   8in

F   E   D   C

e   d

5in   ¼in   5in   ¾in   5in

16in

¼in

1in   GUSSET   3in

5in

5¼in

— — cardboard stiffening
····· pocket position
each square = 1in

▲ *Plan your patterns for the clutch bag and lining from this diagram*

▼ *Putting the gussets in place*

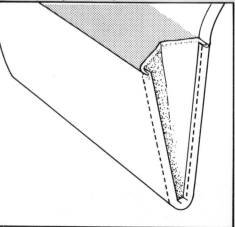

Fold the pocket piece in half as indicated and glue the two sides together to make a piece measuring 5 inches by 3 inches.

Meanwhile, cut out the bag lining from the lining fabric and lining for the gusset pieces, using the pattern.

When the pocket piece is dry, lightly stick it in position as indicated in the diagram and then machine stitch in position on three sides.

Attaching the lining

The lining is now glued to the outside leather, onto the surface of the card interlining, and the gusset lining pieces are

also glued to the gusset pieces. Turn in the edges of lining as you work and smooth it down using the bone folder. When everything is dry, stitch the top edges of the two gusset pieces. Then machine stitch the top edge of the bag (G-F) and all round the flap (ABCD).

Turn the skived edges of the gusset pieces to the right side and turn the skived edges of the bag along lines GHA and FED to the wrong side. Snip at E-e and H-h. Glue and then stitch the gussets into place (diagram 7). If it seems difficult to machine stitch the gussets, they can be sewn by hand.

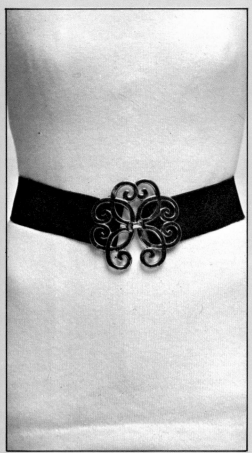

▲ *A simple belt, a beautiful buckle*
▼ *Ways with bright suede*

▲ *Simple bag and belt in appliqué.*
▼ *Belts and purses to make*

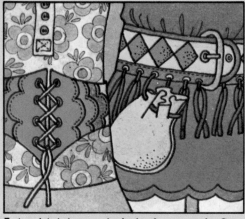

▼ *A quick belt to make in leather or suede. Cut out several shapes and link to waist measurement.*

▲ *Make this gay patchwork jerkin in diamond shapes. Cut a template first and cut sufficient pieces from scraps of suede. Cut out the garment pieces from heavy cotton (use a commercial paper pattern for a jerkin). Lightly glue the diamond shapes in position, just touching. Use a latex adhesive. When the glue is dry, machine stitch the diamond shapes in to position, using a zig zag stitch. Make up the garment as instructed in the pattern.*

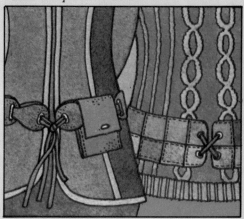

Fasten with buckle or thong.

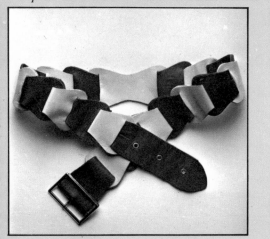

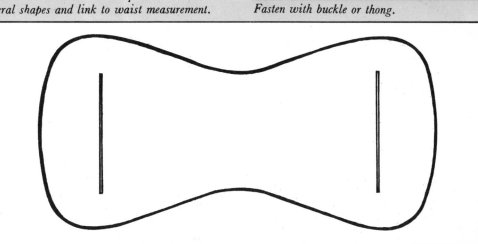

Tie and dye printing

The process and method

Tie and dye is the term given to a process where patterns are dyed into cloth, and it's so simple even a child can do it— and many children do produce beautiful examples.

The craft consists of taking a piece of fabric, then tying, folding, binding, knotting or sewing it so that when the fabric is dipped in a dyebath the colour penetrates the untied areas and a pattern appears on the areas which have been protected from the dye. More complex patterns can be created by using more than one colour, and re-tying first one area, then another. Tie and dye can be worked on lengths of fabric for furnishing, on household linens or on garments. Dresses, blouses, skirts, trousers, ties, pillow cases and curtains, can all be decorated with the tie and dye process.

This dress is particularly attractive as the tie and dye effects have been applied to the bodice fabric only, thus providing a focal point on an otherwise plain garment

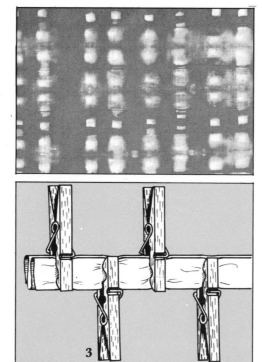

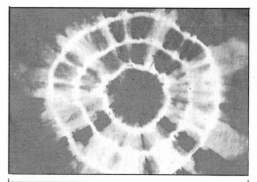

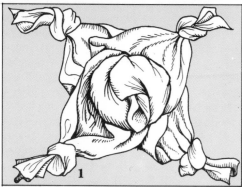

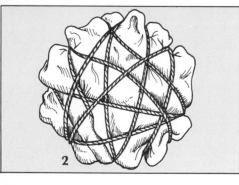

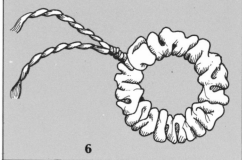

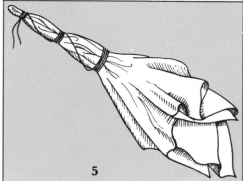

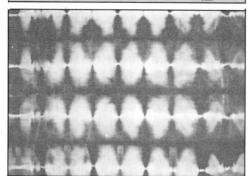

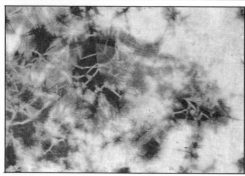

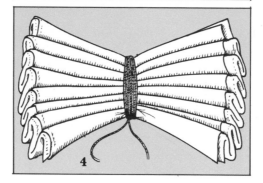

How to make patterns

There are countless ways of tying up a bundle of fabric to produce a design. A picture guide is given in this chapter showing just a few of them and the patterns that will result.

1. Knotted squares. Pick up a point of fabric in the centre of the square, knotting the point and each corner.

2. Marbling. Crumple up the fabric in the hand. Bind into a hard ball. Crumple in different places for each colour used. For a large garment, bunch along the length, section by section, making a long firm roll.

3. Pleat a piece of fabric and secure with clothes pegs.

4. Stripes. Fold a piece of fabric in four, pleat it and then bind with string.

5. Small circle. Pick up a piece of fabric to form a 'furled umbrella' shape and bind with thread.

6. Ruching round cord. Roll a piece of cloth round a length of cord and ruch.

7. Clump-tying. **A.** Bind a cork into a piece of fabric.

8. Clump-tying. **B.** Tie a number of different sized stones into a piece of fabric.

9. Small circle. Pick up a piece of fabric to form a 'flared umbrella' shape and cross bind with thread.

10. Fold a piece of fabric in half and pleat it. Bind at various intervals with string, raffia and thread.

11. Twisting and coiling. Fold the cloth in half, pleat, then twist until it coils back on itself like a skein of wool. Bind at ends and at intervals.

12. Simple double knots.

Experiment and discover which pattern is the most suitable for the fabric or garment being dyed. Marbling makes a pretty, all-over pattern for most things and stripes are particularly effective on towels and curtains.

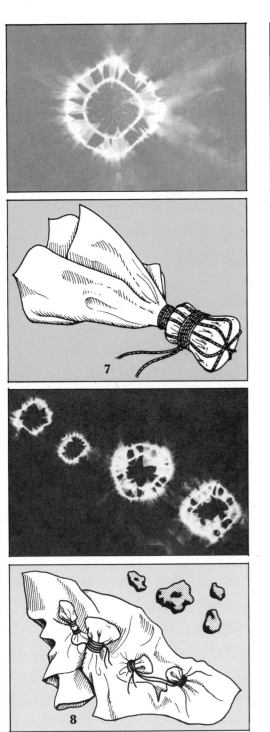

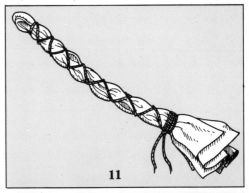

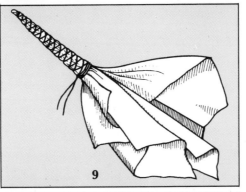

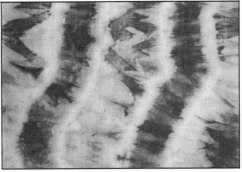

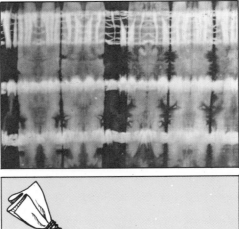

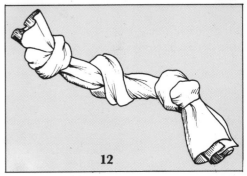

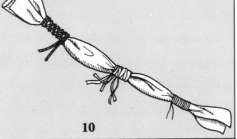

Fabrics and equipment

Cold water dyes will dye natural fibres such as silk, cotton and linen in bright colours. They are very easy to use and the results are wash and light fast. Cold water dyes come in a large range of shades, and one tin of dye is required for each ½lb (250 grams) of dry fabric—ie two to three square yards of medium weight fabric. For example, a dress weighing one pound to be dyed blue and red will require two tins of blue and two tins of red cold water dye.

When fast, cold water dyes are not available a hot dye can be used, but the dyed garment should be laundered separately ever afterwards. Hot dyes are also available in a wide range of colours, and will dye natural and some synthetic fabrics. Simmering will give the intensity of colour intended, but the amount of dye needed and the manufacturer's instructions for hot dyeing should be followed exactly.

Fabrics

It is not advisable to tie-dye woollen sweaters as the tying may make them go out of shape. Woollen fabrics can be dyed but manufacturer's special instructions for dyeing wool should always be followed. Generally, cold dyes are a better choice for woollen fabrics than hot ones.

Fabrics unsuitable for dyeing are polyester/wool mixtures, acrylics (Orlon, Acrilan, Courtelle, Neospun), Tricel and acetate rayon. Fabrics with special finishes resist dyeing and should not be chosen for tie-dyeing. Polyesters, like Terylene, Dacron, and Crimplene, when dyed with triple strength hot dye in dark shades, will come out as pretty pastel shades.

Shirts, linens, towels and anything which is going to need constant washing should be dyed with cold dye, which is colour fast.

Other materials needed

☐ Salt
☐ Soda (for cold dyeing, not needed for hot dyeing)
☐ Wooden spoon to stir with
☐ Rubber gloves to protect hands
☐ Container, big enough to submerge the tied fabric; plastic or glass for cold water dye, a heat resistant container for hot dye
☐ Jug to hold one pint (or half a litre)
☐ Thread, elastic bands, cork, pebbles, string, raffia, cord, cotton, or anything else needed to make the patterns.

Hints and tips

• New fabric may have dressing in it which will resist dye, so boil the garment or fabric first, ironing it smooth again when it is dry.

• When making tie-dyed dresses, always tie-dye the material first, and then make up the dress. The finished garment will have a much more professional look.

• Tie up a sample piece before immersing the whole piece of fabric in the dye bath. Dye, rinse, wash, and untie it, to see whether the resulting pattern and colour is as required. Don't forget that the colour will look darker when the fabric is wet.

• If an old, coloured garment is to be tie-dyed to freshen it, remove the original colour with colour remover, but test a sample first to find out if the dye is fast.

• When two or more colours are used they will blend with one another, so choose colour combinations carefully, remembering that red and blue make mauve; red and yellow make orange; yellow and blue make green; and that a lot of colours mixed together will usually make mud!

How to start

Bind the fabric in any of the ways shown in this chapter. Leave two inches of thread when starting binding, and when binding is completed return to the starting point and tie the two ends together. This will help to ensure that the whole thing does not unravel in the dyebath.

If several bindings are being used on one garment, just use a slip knot and carry the thread onto the next binding.

For a sharp pattern, thoroughly wet the item before putting it in the dye bath. For a softer outline, put the item in the dye bath quite dry.

Prepare the dye. Always work the lightest colour first.

For cold water dyes, dissolve the dye in one pint of warm water, stir well, and pour into the dye container. For each tin of dye used, dissolve 4 tablespoonsful of salt and one tablespoonful of common

▲ *An unusual way of using tie and dyed fabrics.* ▼ *Four neckties to make*

120

soda in one pint of hot water. Stir well, and when everything is ready to dye, add the salt and soda to the mixture. Once the soda is added to the dye, it is only effective for about two hours, so don't add until everything is ready.

Neckties from sheeting
The four ties illustrated were made from tie-dyed cotton sheeting. Experiment with the knots and colours for different effects.

Tortoiseshell banded tie. Dye colours: coral red and café au lait.

Method: Fold a length of cloth 52 inches long by 7 inches wide in half along the length. Tie as many knots along the length as possible. Dye in coral red, rinse, untie, rinse again. Re-tie and dye in café au lait.

Red ovals tie. Dye colours: nasturtium and camellia.

Method: Fold length of cloth 52 inches by 7 inches lengthwise. Pick up small tufts of cloth along the fold and bind them narrowly, leaving a $\frac{1}{4}$ inch gap between each tie. Widen the tufts towards the end. Dye in nasturtium. After rinsing and while still tied, bind each tuft again below the original tie. Dye in camellia.

Purple chevron tie. Dye colours: French navy and camellia.

Method: Cut two pieces of cloth on the cross, each 28 inches by 8 inches. Fold each piece in half lengthwise. Roll the doubled cloth diagonally into a tube, beginning at the corners and working towards the folded edge. Make narrow bindings at 1 inch intervals along this tube. Dye each roll in French navy. Rinse, and while still wet, add further bindings between the original ties. Let the rolls dry and then dye again in weakly-made camellia coloured dye ($\frac{1}{4}$ teaspoonful of dye made up to 1 pint with 2 teaspoonsful of salt and $\frac{1}{4}$ teaspoon of soda added).

Rinse well, hot wash and rinse again. Make up necktie by joining two pieces together and pointing the ends.

Red kipper tie. Dye colour: Camellia.
Method: Cut two lengths of cloth 52 inches by 6 inches. Fold in half lengthwise. Follow this procedure for both pieces, Pick up a piece of fabric, on the fold, about 4 inches from the end. Pull it into a tent shape and bind diagonally right up to the point, then back to the beginning and tie the thread ends. The tent shape by now should be a finger shape. Leave little gaps in the binding so that as the dye partially penetrates a criss-cross texture is achieved. Each of these bindings will make a circle. Make as many circles as required, decreasing in size towards the center. Tie from the other end in the same way. Wet the cloth and dye.

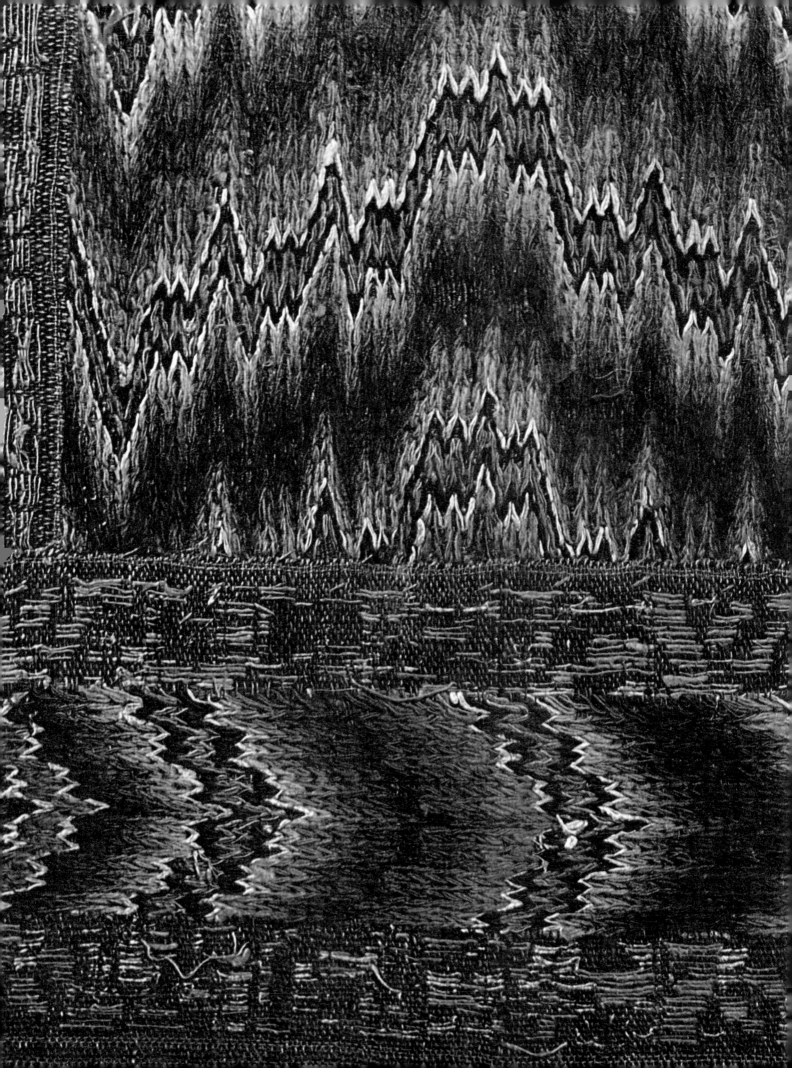

Weaving

An introduction to weaving

Weaving is one of the oldest handcrafts known to man, yet the basic techniques have changed hardly at all since earliest times. It's a craft that almost anyone can master without difficulty, whatever their age—the rag weaving examples shown on this page were worked by children.

Weaving is basically a very simple craft requiring a frame to hold the threads taut so that other threads can be interlaced at right angles.

There are several different kinds of looms and weaving frames available in craft shops. Each of them is designed in a different way to enable the weaver to interlace the yarns in the easiest manner according to the type of fabric to be woven.

The simplest weaving structure of all is a frame card, a piece of card notched at opposite ends with the warp threads strung between them. This will produce small pieces of woven fabric. At the other end of the scale, a beginner can learn to weave on a four-shaft loom with equal

This detail from a woven wall hanging demonstrates the versatility of the craft

▲ *Study this picture of the finished frame loom before starting to make it. You will get a clearer idea of the use of various parts*

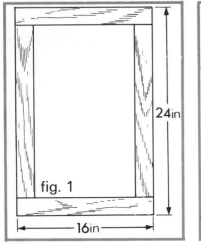

fig. 1

24in

16in

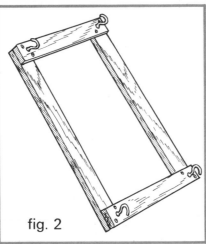

fig. 2

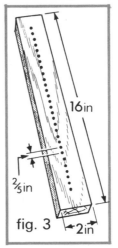

fig. 3

16in

2/5in

2in

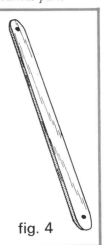

fig. 4

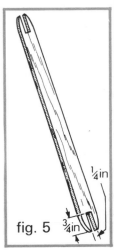

fig. 5

1/4in

3/4in

chances of success, and produce all kinds of woven fabrics for wall hangings, rugs, mats, table runners, clothes and accessories. As an introduction to this fascinating and absorbing craft, this chapter gives instructions for making a simple frame loom and setting it up for weaving, and suggests some ideas for using the woven fabric.

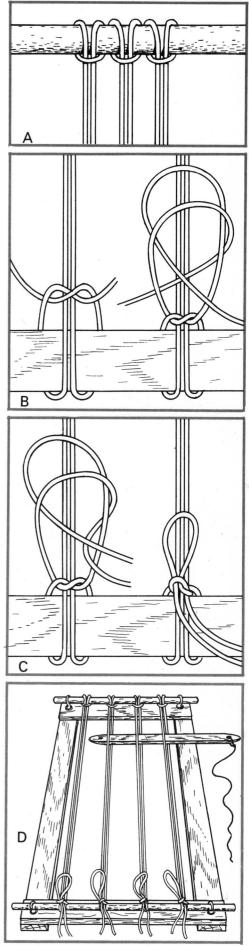

A

B

C

D

Glossary of weaving terms

Warp. Threads stretched lengthwise on a loom.

Weft. The cross threads woven into the warp.

Shed. The wedge-shaped opening, created when alternate warp threads are raised or lowered; the space where the weft yarn travels across the warp.

Raddle. (Sometimes called the 'reed'). A comb-like implement for separating the warp threads and 'beating up' the weft.

Leashes. Strings tied to groups of warp threads, to pull them up to make a shed.

Draft. The way in which the loom is threaded up.

Shed Stick. An implement which, when turned on its side, makes a shed for the weft threads to pass through.

Weaving Stick. The implement upon which the weft yarn is wound and which is used to pass the weft threads through the sheds.

A simple frame loom

To make the loom you will need:
☐ Planed timber 10ft x 2in x 1in
☐ Planed timber 4ft 6in x 1in x ¼in
☐ 3ft of ½in dowelling rod
☐ 4 brass 1¼in hooks
☐ 8 1¼in No. 6 screws
☐ ½lb 2½in round head nails

Constructing the frame
Cut the timber into required sizes:
☐ 3 lengths 16 inches long and 2 lengths 24 inches long from the 2in x 1in timber.
☐ 3 lengths 18 inches long from the 1in x ¼in timber.

Stage 1. Place two 16 inch lengths across two 24 inch lengths to make a frame. Make sure the corners are absolutely square and screw the four pieces together,

using two screws on each corner (figure 1).

Stage 2. Bore a hole in each corner of the frame between the screw heads, using a bradawl. Screw in the hooks so that the open end of the hook faces outwards (figure 2).

Stage 3. Cut the length of dowelling rod in half. This is used to make the rods on which the warp threads are tied. The hooks hold the rods in position (see illustration of completed frame loom).

The Raddle. Draw a line down the center of the remaining 16 inch length of wood. Leaving approximately 1 inch at either end, mark points along the center line at ⅖ inch intervals. Drill ⅛ inch holes approximately ¼ inch deep at each point. Insert a nail in each hole and tap them home until they are firmly embedded. Do not hammer or the wood may split (figure 3).

Shed stick. Take two of the 18 inch lengths of wood and drill an ⅛ inch hole at both ends of each piece, one inch in from the end. Round off and smooth the ends of both pieces (figure 4).

Weaving stick or wooden shuttle. Using the remaining 18 inch length of wood, cut slots into each end 1 inch deep by ¼ inch wide as shown in figure 5.

Setting up the loom

Putting on the warp
Cut warp threads twice the length of the weaving frame (48 inches) plus 10 inches and tie them onto one of the warp rods in the way shown in diagram A, making sure that the ends are of equal length. Space them evenly along the rod.

With a narrow end of the frame towards you, hook the rod into place at the far end of the frame and then tie the warp ends onto the front rod as follows: working from the center take a pair of warp threads and pull them taut over and under the front rod and tie in a single knot as shown in diagram B. This first knot will hold the warp rod in place at the front of the frame while you continue knotting all the warp threads. Make sure that the tension is even. When all the pairs of warp threads are tied, complete the knot as shown in diagram C.

The warp threads are now complete.

Making the first shed. Put the shed stick in position at the top of the frame by sliding it over the first right hand warp thread and under the first left warp thread and working thus across the loom (diagram D). Tie the shed stick with a piece of string through the end holes to prevent it falling out of the loom. When this stick is turned on its side it makes a shed for the weft threads to pass through.

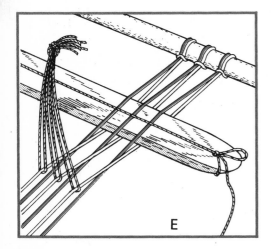

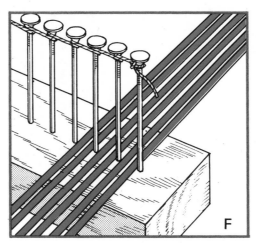

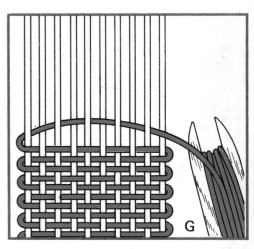

Making the second shed. The second shed is made using leashes and for these use a ball of soft firm string—rough string would damage the warp threads. Cut the required number of strings 18 inches long. Loop a piece of string under one of the right hand warp threads just in front of the shed stick. Knot the ends of the leash together evenly. Knot two more right hand warp threads and then knot the leashes together in groups of three about 4 inches above the warp threads (see diagram E). Tie the remaining leashes across the loom in the same way. The second shed is made by holding the grouped leashes firmly and lifting them so that the weft threads can pass through the space.

Plain weave

To produce a plain weave first one series of warp threads is lifted by turning the shed stick onto its side and then alternate threads are lifted on the groups of leashes. This means that (by counting from the right) the shed stick lifts even numbered warp threads and the leashes lift odd numbered warp threads.

The raddle

The raddle spaces the warp threads evenly and is also used to beat the weft threads into position. Place the raddle on the loom in front of the leashes so that the warp threads go through the spaces between the nails in pairs. Then loop a piece of soft string round each nail to keep the warp ends from jumping out of position (see diagram F). The frame loom is now ready for the weaving to commence.

Yarns

Because the frame loom has a fairly coarse construction, it is better to use a fairly thick yarn for the warp. Thick rug wool or thick soft string would be suitable for the first attempt at weaving. Finer

yarns or mixed textures can be used when a little experience has been gained. It is important when choosing the warp yarn not to use anything that breaks or fluffs too easily.

Suitable weft yarns are cotton, wool, linen and string. For fun and more exciting effects try weaving with strips of paper, grass, rushes, cane, dried plants, lengths of beads, lace, ribbon, pieces of thin wood, or strips of coloured fabric. Remember when using different yarns and colours to exaggerate the contrast to achieve the most interesting results.

Starting to weave

Wind the weft yarn onto the weaving stick, making sure that it does not get too fat because it is then awkward to use. Turn the shed stick onto its side so that it makes a shed and slide the second shed stick through the space in front of the raddle. Holding the raddle parallel with the front of the frame, pull it firmly towards you until it can go no further. By putting the stick in at the beginning of the weaving you make sure that the warp ends lie evenly spaced for making an even textured cloth (see diagram G). You are now ready to begin using the weft yarn, which is passed through so that it lies in an arc on the warp threads and is then beaten evenly into position again at the front shed stick with the raddle. Lift the leashes and pass the weft through the shed. Begin and end weft threads in exactly the same way, by hooking the thread around the outside warp thread.

It is essential to keep the weaving the same width all the time and this is done by making sure that the weft threads are not pulled too tight. This is why the weft threads are left in an arc before being beaten into place and not pulled in a straight line across the cloth.

When the weaving is complete remove the leashes, the shed sticks and the raddle,

untie the half knots at one end and slide the rod from the other end.

Finishing warp thread ends

For mats the ends of the cloth can either be hemmed and fringed or knotted and fringed.

Weaves

On this draft plain weaves are woven but by free weaving (ie lifting the warp threads individually by hand and not using the shed stick and leashes) a greater variety of woven effects can be achieved. Free weaving is used when substances other than yarns are used for the weft.

Things to make

Shoulder bag

Weave brightly coloured stripes of plain weave. Remove the work from the loom and sew up the sides. Fringe the warp ends to make an interesting border at the top of the bag. Add a cord for the handle and line the bag with a firm material. For a different effect, weave an inlay pattern on a plain background. Knot the warp ends together to form a side seam and sew up one side for the base of the bag. Add a handle and line with fabric.

Mats

Make a set of mats in plain weave stripes, varying the combination of colours or textures for each mat. Fringe the edges. Rushes, canes, raffia, or string can be used for interesting textures but remember that the mats must be cleanable.

Wall hangings

One can experiment and use different kinds of yarns and all kinds of objects to make wall hangings because they don't have to withstand wear and tear. If a great deal of colour is required, keep the texture and weave simple. If rich texture is the aim, use very simple colours.

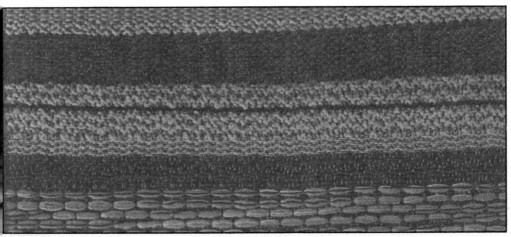

▲ *Fine jute warp, weft of mixed wool and worsted*   ▼ *Plain weave, 4 thin warp threads woven as one*

Some of the things which can be made with the fabric woven on the frame loom

▲ *Plastic warp; lace, wool, rayon, tassels weft*   ▼ *Pattern here made by free darning on weaving*

Collector's Pieces

Some of the illustrations used to introduce our crafts are of great interest, both historically and technically. Details are given below.

Page 12

The detail illustrated is from a painting by the fifteenth century Italian artist Piero della Francesca. Medieval ladies of high birth often wore elaborate bead jewellery and the subject was probably wearing her best pieces for the portrait. On her head is displayed a gold jewelled ornament threaded with ribbon; around her neck is a heavy looking collar with a medallion pendant, while another piece, equally elaborate, is pinned to the braided coil of hair over her ear. The picture now hangs in the Uffizi Gallery, Florence.

Page 18

In the early nineteenth century the creation of bead pictures was a popular craft and looms were usually handmade from wooden or cardboard boxes. The loom on which 'Townscape' was worked was constructed from an old cigar box.

Page 36

The art of enamelling can be traced back many centuries. The master of the Louis XII triptych illustrated consist of nine Limoge panels and was made in France between 1499 and 1514. Enamels were painted onto copper in the traditional manner. Gilding was added as a final touch. Louis XII and St. Louis are shown on the left, the Annunciation in the centre, and Anne of Bretagne and St. Anne on the right.

Page 42

This beautiful casket was bequeathed to the Victoria and Albert Museum in London by Sir Frederick Richmond. On the lid, the date 1678 has been worked into the embroidery, followed by the initials E.C., ascribed to Elizabeth Coombe. The casket, lined with pink silk and fitted with numerous compartments, also has a mirror edged in silver braid inside the lid. The exterior, a detail of which we show, is upholstered in white satin and embroidered with coloured silks in a variety of stitches that include long and short, split, Rococco, tent, needlepoint, fillings and knots, with laid, couched, raised and detached work added for textural interest. Details have been emphasised with silk tapestry, beads and seed pearls.

Page 92

This exquisite eighteenth century bedspread is made up of square and triangular shaped pieces of satins, brocades and velvets. These have been embroidered with silver gilt threads and coloured silks in satin, stem, long and short and chain stitches with couched applied work. Some of the squares have appliquéd pictures illustrating scenes from Aesop's fables. The pieces of silk incorporated in the bedspread date from periods throughout the eighteenth century. Some are even earlier.

Page 120

Persia has always been famous for its beautiful carpets. The craft reached the peak of its perfection in technique, colour and design during the sixteenth century. The Chelsea carpet illustrated is a particularly fine example and was discovered in the King's Road, London and bought by the Victoria and Albert Museum in 1890. The texture is extremely fine, achieved by working more than 45 knots to each square inch, and since the Chelsea carpet measures 17′ 8″ by 9′ 8″ one can only feel a sense of awe and adoration for craftsmen with such patience and endurance.

Page 122

This detail is from a much larger panel worked in the eighteenth century as part of a set of hangings. These were much in vogue for a time as a cheap imitation of tapestry but by 1740 they were out of fashion. Woven in wool and linen on a hemp warp and weft, the design imitates Hungarian Point or flame stitch and closely resembles Florentine embroidery. The panel is accredited to a weaver, Pierre Maille, whose name is worked into the edge of the fabric. It is known that he lived in Elbeuf in Northern France and inherited his father's looms in 1732, thus making this particular panel one of the latest of the period. It now hangs in the Victoria and Albert Museum, London.